THE PERSECUTION OF OTHERS

When the others are you who will help you then?

Justine Linden and

Samantha Flower LLB (Hons)

The Persecution of Others

When the others are you who will help you then?

By

Justine Linden and

Samantha Flower LLB (Hons)

Table of Contents

<u>Disclaimer for Spelling</u>

When choosing whether to write the story using the American English or U.K. English, Samantha and I found it difficult to decide, after all we have been brought up in both systems and experienced both cultures. So we decided that the spelling was not as important as the story itself just as long as it does not disturb the reader so much that they can't finish the book. Some words are spelt in American English and some in the original Queens English and I hope for the purists of Language and Literature this is not too much of a problem. As Samuel Clements has so often been referenced on this matter, "I have little respect for a man who only knows how to spell a word one way." I guess for a dyslexic these words are golden.

Justine Linden

ACKNOWLEDGEMENTS

To Rev. Lawrence Farley, the greatest thanks for all of your support and spiritual guidance throughout our lives. To our principal (of V.C.H.S) Mr. Gerard Giguere, without your leadership this journey would have had a very different ending. To all the teachers and staff of V.C. for the bravery and love they showed the child. To the late Mr. Sean Burke, who took on this burden on his own, thank you. To the late Mr. Don Hastings, his love and gift of teaching will never be forgotten; you will be in our hearts forever. To Mrs. Sharon Meehan, you were the first to understand the child Justine, besides her sister and believed in her and gave her the tools to learn. To our childhood friend and V.C. brother Steve Karmazenuk, who guided us through the journey of writing and publishing. To Dieter Halbwidl, for all of your insight and help in editing. To our big sister Kim Davis, for guiding us through puberty and leading us astray, oh, the memories! But that shall be another book. To all our friends who have supported us with this book. To Garry Marsh for helping with the front cover with his photography skills. And above all to God, who entrusted in us this journey of suffering which enabled us to write such a beautiful story.

Justine Linden and Samantha Flower

This work is registered with the UK Copyright Service:

Registration No:340415

Some names have been changed to protect identities.

persecutionofothers@hotmail.co.uk

www.facebook.com/persecutionofothers

Preface

This is not just the story of a young girl feeling oppressed because of her language, culture and disability. It is a journey that at some point most human beings will endure. You may say this happened to a girl because she is dyslexic or because she is English so therefore it is not something that I can relate to. So I say to you, "This has been you, it will be you and it can be you." At some point you may find yourself to be out of place in this world and oppressed or persecuted for it, because you are the wrong class, colour, religion, culture, sex, sexuality, political persuasion, physical appearance or disability and it is then that this journey has become yours. "The Persecution of Others", you are the others. For those of you when reading this, that know that you are one of the others; let this journey be yours and may you find peace through it.

THE PERSECUTION OF OTHERS

(I)

I confess that I do feel the difference of mankind, national and individual... I am, in plainer words, a bundle of prejudice-made up of likings and disliking.

Charles Lamb

Vaudreuil Catholic High School (V.C.H.S.) 1986

I'm 14 years old, puberty hasn't quite kicked in for me yet, I was one of those late bloomers. I'm not alone though, sitting next to me is my identical twin sister Samantha, who is also flat-chested and looks about ten, which of course is devastating at that age. The boys in our year enjoyed calling us the "flat-chested ones" and used to ask us to go work-out on our pectorals. It wasn't just Sam and me, there was my sister's best friend at the time Karen, she got all the comments too; it was of course a part of growing up I guess. It's early September and I am in grade nine also known as secondary three. I am a student at Vaudreuil Catholic High School (V.C.H.S.). Which is in Vaudreuil, just off the western edge of Ile Perrot of Montreal, Quebec, Canada to those of you that don't know the area that well. I'm in the middle of Moral Education class, taught by Brian Connolly, a very gentle laid back man who never raised his voice or lost his temper in the whole time I saw him teach at that school. He is a slim build man, about five foot six with auburn hair and he has a thick moustache. He's about to introduce to me a book that is so profound that it will change the way I will see the world and all of mankind for the rest of my life.

Mr. Connolly, "Today we are going to start reading a book about a man who survived a Nazi concentration camp it's called "Man's Search for Meaning" by Victor E Frankl." You all get a book and I want you to continue reading it at home as homework and at the end of the month you're going to write a paper on it."

The whole of the class begins to whine and whinge including me. The reason we're all here doing Moral Education (M.E.) is because most of us have convinced our parents that we shouldn't have to do Religious Education at all because either we're not Catholic and therefore we should not have to be subjected to their dogma and rhetoric or we are Catholic and we're sick of being told that we are all sinners and we will burn in hell. Not all of our teachers held this view of us being sinners and burning in hell. Most were laid back fun loving souls; that I am sure in their time had done their fair share of sinning. This had so far worked for the past two years for us gang of rebels and got us a free period almost every week while all our other peers had to endure Religious Education (R.E.). This year the powers that be had decided that due to the increased numbers of students that were dropping out of R.E. they needed to replace it with another subject so they came up with Moral Education. It would replace the credits we would be losing and teach us something about morals, joy for us.

Mr. Connolly, "Six million Jews were killed in the second world war, they were put in concentration camps along with Roman Gypsies, homosexuals and other minority groups; we now refer to this as the Holocaust. Victor E Frankl was a psychiatrist and a psychotherapist and had his entire world taken from him, including his wife and yet he managed to survive the concentration camp experience and rebuild his life afterwards. He went on to write a book about his experience as an inmate in the camps and how he managed to survive when others perished."

Mr. Connolly started reading the first few paragraphs then the book is passed on to each pupil, starting with my twin Sam. The book is never passed on to me and there is a good reason for that, I can't read. I just sit there listening to the words of this man Victor and begin to take in his horrific and tragic story, his journey in life that he managed to survive. Just when I thought my life had been crap, I was now finding out that this man's life and millions more had been destroyed. Their families murdered, they had been tortured and treated like something less valuable than a cockroach. For a moment the world in me stopped and became very quiet as I listened to the truth, it was the beginning of an epiphany. The bell rang we're told to read up to page fifty at home and we'll pick it up from there next week.

I get home that afternoon and fix myself a snack in the kitchen, which I take back to my bedroom. I share my bedroom with my twin sister Sam and I find her on her bed lying on her back with the book held up in the air reading. I ask her to read it to me. She gives me that look, like I'm a pain in the arse and breathes out of her nose like a kind of huff because she's already half way through the book and doesn't want to have to start again for me. So I give her my look, which means I'm not going to leave it and so she obliges. I sit down on the floor with my back against the side of her bed and listen to her read. I make Sam read to me almost half the book, every time she would stop and say "that's enough now, let me read on my own." I insist she reads on until I've had enough and want to go away and think about what I've heard. Human beings had been murdered like they were dirtier and less valuable than rats and bugs, millions of them. That night in my bed I laid there and thought about them all and cried.

The following week in M.E. we pick the book up at about page fifty of *"Experiences in a concentration Camp"* and continue through for another ten pages. Mr. Connolly then opens discussion on what we have read. It's clear by the discussions and arguments debated that in the class you have a mix of those who have read further on in the book and even finished it, (like Sam who finished it that night when we got home) and those who haven't bothered to read a thing since they were last in class. Some things never change with students there are those who do and those who won't. You will always get a mix of children in any class, there are the ones at the front of the class that are so enthusiastic and want to learn it all, bless them; those in the middle taking it all in but not wanting to be too noticed and those at the back hiding who are just not interested. I was a strange character, I wanted to take it all in every last drop but I didn't want the world to know I couldn't read or write. I needed to sit next to my sister wherever she was sitting so that she could help me to prevent anyone from finding out. One of the reasons why I was able to slip through the system without being noticed was the fact that the teachers here had a policy of not forcing children to read out loud if they didn't feel comfortable with it. That was used to what I mistakenly thought was my advantage. As the debate was winding down in class Mr. Connolly asked the class a question, till the day I die, I will never forget it, what he asked us all.

"Why was this able to happen? Why were we able to kill and destroy so many people without anyone standing up and saying that it was not acceptable?"

The class went quiet with thought, I heard myself just say it.

"When we reduce people to nothing, less than a bug we can do whatever we want with them, killing them is easy then".

That was my epiphany. My sister turned to me and smiled she had figured this out when she was about eight years old. But that's a story for later. Mr. Connolly turned and looked at me and repeated what I said almost verbatim

"When we reduce people to nothing, less than a bug we can do whatever we want with them, is exactly what they did to the Jews and others they didn't want".

Mr. Connolly continues, "They first destroyed them by making everyone believe that they were not the same as them; they are greedy, they are not as clean as you, they are not as intelligent as you, they are devious, they are evil and dangerous. They are not a productive part of the society that you value and are dragging it down and they are causing all of the problems in society. That is what the Nazi's needed to do first, make them less than human and they used propaganda and pseudo-science to help them do this".

One of the students at the back shouts up. "Why do we need to be learning about this now since it was years ago, it's the past, why can't we just forget about it?" Connolly looks to the back of the class at the boy and says "we should learn about it to make sure that it never happens again in the future, by learning what we did wrong and how it happened"

The boy retorts. "Well the world has learnt; it won't happen again we won't repeat that mistake."

Now it's Sam's turn. "Oh really ay, you think the world couldn't do it again we're not that far off it here in Quebec."

The boy calls out in disbelief, "What?"

Sam argues back, "do you really think we're much better here in Quebec right now? And what about the history of North America itself, what happened to the Native Americans and don't get me started on the black Africans. This has been going on since man began and will continue for a long time yet, it's not the first and it won't be the last holocaust."

The bell rings we all grab our books to leave, the discussion is over.

The discussion and my sister's argument stay with me as I start to think about Quebec and my life here since we left England. I am a child hiding in an English school that I am not allowed by law to be in because I am different to the rest of the children. Sam and I both, and no other student in this school are aware of this. We are landed immigrants in Canada. The story goes that two weeks before we landed in this province the last of the English signs were taken down and it became French only. The truth is I don't know when the last of the English signs came down because I wasn't there and didn't arrive here until the summer of 1981, in the middle of all of Quebec's disputes with the English legacy that appeared to have done a lot of damage to the French people, which in-turn was now affecting the English speaking people. The French people of Quebec felt that they had been continuously undermined by the English and treated like second class citizens in this province and yet they made up the majority. They felt that they had been treated like the lower class in what should have been a classless society. The province was institutionally bigoted against the French majority. It was no longer a bi-lingual province and according to the French it had never been. They had been the underdogs for a very long time and it had built up a tremendous amount of resentment and hatred towards the English speaking minority, so much so that there had been rioting, bombings, kidnappings and murders by the time we got to Quebec. This was not a province at peace; it was a province at war with itself, with the inequality that had been going on for far too long. And maybe it's time to tell this story so that the world can know the truth. That if you oppress one person in this world, or a group of people because you are threatened by them, or feel superior or just because you don't agree with their beliefs, or like the language they speak, or even the color of their skin, that you are sowing seeds of resentment and hatred. They will grow to be dangerous and filled with rage and revenge and you will reap what you have sown. If not yourself be a victim of your own undoing but your children or grandchildren will be and they will be left to have to repair the damage, and sometimes those wounds can be so deep it may feel like it can never be repaired.

French was now the only language to be accepted in Quebec. This law is known as Bill 101 (Loi 101) this is the Charter of the French Language (La charte de la langue française) of 1977 it defines French as the only official language of Quebec. Fundamental language rights for everyone in the province were changed. It meant every road sign was changed to French, all advertisements were in French, when you went in a shop they spoke to you in French first and most of the time they would only speak to you in French or you would not be served. All business, the civil services and public transport must now fundamentally operate in French. It was like another France but with an undercurrent of resentment and even hatred for what they believed had been done to them. It is the central legislative piece in Quebec's language policy but it did not stop there, it also meant that children like me from another country were not allowed by law to go to an English school. They were required by law to attend French schooling only. I was one of the children of Bill 101. So here I was breaking the law, being educated in an English school along with my sister Sam but we weren't alone in this, every teacher in this school was involved including the principal and secretaries. This carried a prison sentence for anyone found breaking the law.

There are no accidents in this world. I don't think my teachers had just happened to choose the book *"Man's Search for Meaning"* for us to read by accident nor the book after that *"*Anne Frank, *The Diary of a Young Girl"* just for the sake of it. The other children in the class knew nothing of what was going on in the school with us and they probably still to this day don't know, but those books, at the time were poignant. These books were also inspiring me to want to be able to read them on my own and not have to be at the mercy of my twin.

I wanted desperately to be able to pick up these books and spend some time alone with them and take them in, in my own time.

I remember when Sam first read Anne Frank to me I had no idea that she was dead. I had assumed that because she was the one writing the diary, like Victor, she had survived. When it dawned on me what my sister was reading, I was in shock and I began to cry. Later that night my sister heard me crying while I lay in my bed, with my small body facing the wall and she whispered to me from across our bedroom

"Justine, she is in heaven now, she'll be ok. She is with God and I know how you feel. I cried too the first time I found out".

I prayed to God that night for a sister I had just found and then lost before I got the chance to know her.

These two characters, Victor and Anne were heroes, they had an inner bravery that quietly shone out and yet there were no other heroes around to save them from what they were going through. They were on their own, trying their best to stay alive on a day to day basis and as we all know now only Victor managed to survive, Anne was not so fortunate. So here I was, as a young girl thinking, could I ever dare to be so brave when it counted in my life? Even at the moment of asking myself that, I knew that I probably wasn't. To admit illiteracy was not an easy thing to do and I had yet to face up to that. Never mind being able to take a stand against being persecuted or for that matter standing up for any of your fellow human beings that are being persecuted. I would have to admit that I had cheated to have got this far with the whole illiteracy issue. What kid would put their neck on the line and admit so much and therefore put myself at the mercy of others. And what if they can't help me anyway, what if it's gone on for far too long to save me now? Then what do I do?

So here I am at my sister's mercy not only does Sam, have to read these books to me she has to help me write my paper. Although this is a frustrating and exhausting process for the both of us it leads us into a discussion on persecution in its many forms and how our own lives have been affected by it.

1984

École Secondaire De La Cité-Des-Jeunes

(II)

"Before you embark on a journey of revenge, dig two graves."

Confucius

It is late in the summer of 1984, in Quebec and we have recently moved to the suburbs of Pincourt where my parents have bought their first house here and they are so happy, we all are. It is more out in the countryside not so built up compared to the north shore of Pointe-Claire where we had just moved from. I was glad to be out of there because I had been forced to go to a French primary school and had become very unhappy, even suicidal at times. I was deeply depressed because I had learning difficulties and the French school Saint Louis was not equipped with the knowledge or the skills to deal with an English child that was suffering and struggling in this way. Louise, our teacher was very compassionate and understanding but soon realized that I was more than she could deal with. The school councilor Guy was a fantastic man that I will always remember with fondness but even he could not help me. I am severally dyslexic, which is something I am deeply ashamed of and try to hide every day of my life. I have wished my brain would just fix itself and set me free. I have tremendous trouble with learning any language even my own native tongue has been an unbelievable struggle. The school previous to this one, Saint Jude, had helped me a great deal. However, putting me in a French school was about to send me further backwards and all that had been done to help me in Saint Jude School was going to be undone. Not just academically but psychologically and emotionally. It was going to cause severe arrested development and add to my already overwhelming emotional difficulties and low self-esteem. This is devastating to a child of eleven that would soon be going off to high school.

They had a different set of problems with Samantha; she had refused to learn French but instead learnt Spanish from Nancita and her family who lived next door to us in Pointe-Claire. They were a lovely family that enjoyed teaching Sam

Spanish. They originated from Central America and somehow managed to cross two boarders the United States and then the Canadian in hope of achieving a better life for their family. There had been in the past decade a mass exodus of Anglophones (English speaking Canadians) from Quebec, which made the way for the next generation of Allophones (one whose mother tongue is neither English nor French). They were a trilingual family that were fluent in Spanish their native tongue, then French and English, that to me is a wonderful gift and they were a pleasure to know. Nancita went to the same school as us and she did her best to teach me French but it just wasn't going in, not for lack of trying on her part or mine. The principal (Le director) of Saint Louis wasn't very impressed with our behavior; that would be the fighting and the disregard for the rules and Sam's refusal to learn French, and my truancy. Le director brought us in for a chat. Samantha was asked by him why she refused to learn their language and insisted on speaking Spanish?

Samantha began her argument. "Firstly, it is my right to chose to speak the language I wish to speak, that should be my basic human right, and secondly, you can't force me to speak the language that you want me to speak, and thirdly, because you don't know how to teach it."

"You are failing immigrant students".

"You have put laws in-place to stop us from learning English but no facilities in-place to help us children from other countries to learn French; you just expect us to jump in and catch-up with the rest of you half way through. There is no special support or classes for us children from England or any other country to help us settle and learn in a supportive environment starting with the basics like you would a baby. Therefore our overall education is then suffering because of this".

"I learned Spanish from my neighbors next door because they taught me the same way they taught their baby daughter". "So what do you expect from us?"

Le director explained to Samantha that things were not going to be working out for her for much longer, if she didn't change her attitude because next year she would be going to Saint Thomas' secondary school and that it was most likely that we would both be forced to repeat grade six, if things didn't improve. We had been on a day visit to Saint Thomas' and the teachers there seemed very sympathetic towards us and had said that they would do what they could to help. They were aware of my learning difficulties, but le director was right, we did need to try a lot harder for our own sakes.

The following week we were given special classes with Louise, to learn French starting with the basics. Louise also recommended that we watch Passe-Partout, which was the Québécois answer to Sesame Street. Passe-Partout is the by-product of the Quebec minister of education in 1970 after considering the translation of Sesame Street into Québécois French, however due to the belief held at the time that the French Canadian children would not be able to relate to an American children's program. This project was born and handed over in 1973 to the producer Laurent Lachance. The irony of this is due to Lachance's differences' with his employers Radio-Quebec, Passe-Partout didn't air until 1977 while the Québécois version of Sesame Street first aired in 1975.

Our individual tuition with Louise didn't last long though, Sam started learning French, and I just became withdrawn and eventually, I started running away from school again. One of the issues that had pushed me over the edge was that the English teacher from the school had called my mother up to explain that she had requested that I was to be put into the other English group, because of my learning difficulties. That I was so far behind in English, that she could not help me, and that I would be better off in the other group. By the other group she meant with the French children that could hardly speak a word of English, that were struggling with the basics, like cat and dog, and hi my name is Jean-Guy, that group. That's how bad my English was, never mind my French. There was a Middle English group but my English wasn't good enough for that group.

My life at that point had hit an all-time low; I could not even manage to stay in the higher English group with the French kids. I hated my mind, I hated my life and I hated myself. My mother begged her not to do it to me. She said that separating me from my sister and putting me in another group, would not help. It would do me more harm and it would set me even further back in my education. My mother both begged and insisted that they didn't do this to me, but the damage was done. I had heard the conversation and I knew what this woman was saying was true. I could not read or write in

English either; I was sinking in both directions, French and English.

The school found out that I was taking off and spending my days here there and everywhere like the mall and the local wooded area near our house. Guy, the school's councilor, told me if I didn't want to come to school they would rather I stayed at home with my mother, where I would be safe and not hiding out, God knows where. So I agreed to stay at home when I didn't want to go to school, which was most days. It was a blessing that they let me stay at home because I was sick of hiding in the woods during the day. You would not believe the amount of adults and teenagers that were going in there just to have sex, all kinds of sex, heterosexual sex and homosexual sex. It was like a secret sex hive. Don't worry, it's not like these people were putting on a show for me, they weren't aware that I was even there. I would hide up in the trees and just live and play inside my own mind, most of the time. I was on another planet with Captain James T. Kirk and Spock and the gang dealing with bigger more pressing issues, like Universal galactic peace and green chicks with two belly-buttons that Kirk liked more than me. I had a crush, what can I say, it's the truth, it soon switched to Spock though, I prefer more emotionally elusive men now; they're more of a challenge. These trees were the best for climbing. It felt like the branches were powerful arms that cradled my frail body from this world that was just too much for me. They captured my imagination and were ideal for making a tree-house. All I needed was some wood and something to make a roof out of and I could have moved right in there and never had to go home again, and more importantly, I would never have had to go back to school. Mind you, sometimes the noises they would be making down there would bring me back to reality but then at least the noises meant it was soon over, especially the heterosexual ones, once the guy made that grunt it was over and I could go back to my adventures with the gang and captain Kirk.

Note to self don't hide in trees close to big sunken in areas with a dirty old mattress dumped in it. So to be honest I was better off at home watching cartoons and drawing my strawberry shortcake characters. Sam was progressing very well in the school without me; bar from the trouble I got her into for covering up for me every time I skipped school. She was probably doing much better without me there dragging her down asking her all the time to do my work for me. At least one of us had a chance of surviving this.

By the end of the academic year our parents had decided to move to Pincourt, they had finally found a house they wanted to buy. This changed everything; it meant that we would be going to another school instead. Before we left, le director called our mother Julie and told her that he had spoken to le director of the French high school that we would be going to and that the director of the high school would not be tolerating Sam's behavior and that he was going to make an example out of her. He explained as best he could that this director was not an English sympathizer.

It was late in the summer in Pincourt, September was just around the corner and my mother had made an appointment to go and see this director and sort out the details of Sam and me going to the French high school in Vaudreuil (École Secondaire De La Cité-Des-Jeunes). I remember before leaving, my mother putting on her make-up and perfume and dressing her long dark brown hair by back brushing it and using lots of hair spray. The sun light shining through her bedroom window made her hair shimmer. It was so different to mine, sleek and straight not a hint of a curl, a wave or frizz.

My mother had these deep dark brown eyes that matched her brown hair and olive skin. She looked more Native American than British. I thought my mother was the most beautiful woman in the world and whenever we went anywhere she made an effort to look her best. Despite it being as many as twenty years on, whenever I smell her perfume on another woman, it always pulls me straight back to her bedroom, back in Pincourt, with me still sat on her bed watching her getting ready. Smells are like emotional time machines, that only they have control over the destination, we are simply the transfixed and overwhelmed passengers that have been hijacked back to that place that leaves you feeling vulnerable and wanting of that simpler time in your life once more. We took a taxi and arrived there mid afternoon, by taxi the high school is only about 12 minutes from our house in Pincourt.

Le director met us in the corridor outside his office he shook my mother's hand and showed us through to his office and closed the door. He began by explaining to my mother that our grades, especially mine, were not adequate to get a child into high school. That I needed to remain in primary French school and go back to the second grade because I had not been able to grasp the basics in French or even English for that matter. I was devastated hearing that. I thought there is no way I'm going back with kids half my age to learn French. I would rather die. He then went on to say, my sister needed to repeat the last year of primary school before he would accept her in his school. He was looking straight at Sam as he said this. This was worse than what we all expected. The hate in this man could not be disguised. He was of course enjoying this. My mother burst into tears; to be honest she was not alone. I had already started to shed tears quietly with my head bowed low, when he said that I had to remain in primary school for many more years.

Julie asked him, "Why does Samantha need to repeat the year when she is able to speak French now, and has past her last year?"

Le Director responds, "It will do her some good, she needs to learn a more important lesson, about respect of authority."

He continues, "I know from le director of your former school that Samantha had learnt Spanish in a very short time and that her refusal to learn French was nothing more than a political protest. Samantha needs to learn that political activism and protests will not be tolerated here".

Sam responded with frustration in her voice, "You can't punish me for this. It's your fault you can't teach immigrants your language properly and this is just an act of revenge because we are from England. You are persecuting us because you believe the English once persecuted you".

Julie is trying to negotiate other options with him by asking, if it was possible, if he knew of an English high school that would be more understanding of her children's situation because she didn't want Sam and me to be separated. She tried to explain to him that we needed to be kept together for my sake that I was not strong enough to be left without my sister. He told us that there was an English high school on the same campus but he said, "You will not have much luck with him I can assure you of that." He laughed at our mother, a smug laugh that belongs to a man that has crushed his pitiful enemies.

My mother is pleading. "Can you call him anyway and ask him if he would at least see us, please".

She was really crying now and it began to feel hopeless. I just wanted to curl up in a ball and die because there was no way I could survive what he was going to do to me. Separate me from my sister and put me with children half my age to try and learn a language that to me was impossible. What people don't understand is that I would give anything to be able to speak French and fit in. I would have done anything to speak English properly and be able to read and write; it was not a choice for me. I was trapped in my own personal hell. I was trapped inside a mind that would not function right and was failing me and there was nothing I could do about it. He called the English high school on the campus while we were there because my mother was so insistent and he spoke French only to the principal over the phone but by his body language and tone it didn't seem to be going in our favor. He came off the phone and said, "Monsieur Giguere will see you but I would not get your hopes up."

On the way out my sister began to have an exchange of words with him and I remember her calling him a bigoted separatist Nazi bastard and saying, "don't worry I'm leaving and I won't be back." My mother and I left in tears and Sam looked ready for a fight. We walked across the campus to the English side, to Vaudreuil Catholic High School.

We entered in the big front doors of the English high school. To the right you could just see the sectaries office and headed in that direction. In the corridor we could hear the typewriters tapping away, my mother cleared her throat to announce that we were there. The ladies in the office looked up and one of them said "can I help you?" and my mother replied "yes please, we have come to see the headmaster, Mr. Giguere". The lady replied, "of course please take a seat" and pointed to some plastic chairs outside the office. We sat down; my mother and I are still drying our tears. She then went into the door next to her office and spoke to someone in French. When she came out of the office, she smiled at us and said that Mr. Giguere would be with us shortly. Mr. Giguere came out of his office and introduced himself to us, shook my mother's hand and invited her into his office. Mr. Gerard Giguere was of medium build, with pale white skin and white hair brushed back like that of a mad scientist. His strong jaw line and white straight teeth and a smile that naturally came from within made him attractive. His demeanor was calm and controlled yet you knew he would be a force to be reckoned with. He wore horn-rimmed glasses and he tended to wear a lot of light grey suits with dark shirts, I guess they suited his hair and complexion.

They were in there for some time talking. Sam and I were left out in the corridor, just sat there wondering what was going to happen to us, if he would even help us at all. Finally, my mother came out of the office followed by Mr. Giguere and Sam and I stood up to ask what was happening. Our mother addresses us saying, "He would like to talk to both of you on his own".

Mr. Giguere then follows by saying, "Justine and Samantha would you please come with me. I would like to have a chat with you both."

I remember his office had two doors to it on opposite sides of the room. We sat in the chairs across from his big desk and he was sat back in his chair looking at us. Sam looked at me and me at her. I was scared because I didn't know what was going to happen and I remember Sam saying, don't worry, I'll do the talking. Sam knew that I don't know how to talk to adults properly. That it makes me get my words mixed up and stutter and I get confused.

Mr. Giguere began by addressing Sam and he asked her why she had chosen to learn Spanish and had refused for some time to learn French. Sam's response was probably not what he was expecting.

"Because I feel we are being persecuted by the Parti Québécois, they have taken our basic rights away from us just for being English".

"They feel that just because they have been so badly treated by the English over here for so long that it has given them the right to persecute all the English and anyone else who may stand in their way of revenge".

Mr. Giguere, "Revenge?"

Sam responds, "Yes revenge, this is retribution. Bill 101 does not bring equality to the French, it is just a tool to punish the English, they don't want to be treated equally to the English and be given equal life opportunities. They want the English to suffer like they feel they have suffered. They want the English to feel like they are worthless, inferior and not important to Quebec. Just like they believe the English have made them feel. If you wanted equality there would be two languages spoken and written freely here not a law to prevent one. You're destroying your own province and your own people. You're letting your children down in both French and English".

"Your schools should be one, not a school for the French and another next door for the English, both languages should be taught together, with the children growing up in the classrooms together learning that they are no different from each other, that they are equal and are brothers and sisters of Quebec. Not enemies that are separated by language. The English children can survive this for the most part because once they are grown up, if they don't like it, they can move out of the province and get a job anywhere in any corporation in Canada or the world for that matter, but the French children that have not learnt English sufficiently, where can they go? To exist outside of Quebec and survive in the rest of North America and the world, they need English, they can of course move to France but that is about their lot and even in France they would be more of an asset if they were bi-lingual for the International corporate world that we are living in today. Think about it, the rest of the world is moving closer together, wanting to become united in policies that serve all, as a global state, which of course is fuelled by capitalism and Quebec wants to separate from the rest of Canada. Quebec is actually moving in the opposite direction to the rest of the western world. "

"Tell me this, how do you think God feels about all of this, seeing his children fight like this, hurting each other for what? The sake of language which is nothing more than a form of communication, we are all God's children, whatever our language or culture is. Language was given to us to communicate, not to divide us or segregate us. We should live in a world that allows us to speak as many languages as we choose. If you were a Nazi back in Nazi Germany when they were persecuting the Jews, would you rise up against them, your fellow comrades and put your head on the block to save them, or would you stand there and do nothing and watch them all die?"

Mr. Giguere sat back in his chair fixed on Sam and said "do you think that the Parti Québécois are Nazi's?"

Sam argues her case. "Do you not think that there is a fine line when you choose to persecute that can so easily be crossed, where will this persecution end?" "When you choose to take that path to punish those who you feel, have done you such wrong, who is there to stop you from going too far? It's a slippery slope."

Mr. Giguere, "A slippery slope you say, hum."

Sam replies in a more pleading manner now. "Even if you don't take me which I would understand because I can already speak, read and write some French even if the director has his way with me and puts me back a year, I'll come back the next year stronger and they will be so sick of me they will have to move me up a grade; I'm smart I could do high school in two years anyway, but Justine won't survive this. She needs help so please take her and help my sister at least save my sister. I promise you, if you save Justine, I will learn French properly and become perfectly bilingual and I won't cause you any trouble as I have in other schools."

Mr. Giguere asks her, "What will you do with your life?"

Sam replies, "I want to go to university and study people, politics, economics, history and law and one day work in government, that's my dream but I need you to help my sister first."

As my sister speaks for me like this, I bow down my head in shame of what I am. Mr. Giguere sits very quietly looking at us, he then gets up out of his chair and leaves the room from the other door. He is gone a few minutes and then returns with a man and introduces him to us.

"Samantha and Justine, I would like to introduce to you Mr. Larry Farley."

In unison Sam and I say, "Hello".

To this day, this man is one of the most beautiful souls I have ever met in all of my life. He was a tall, medium to slim build African-Canadian, with the most gentle and spiritual demeanor. He had these gorgeous soft eyes and a smile that wasn't a charmer but at peace, it was just his soul. He is the man that walks in a room and his mere presence has the power to liberate others and put you at ease. And his presence in mine and Sam's life has had a profound effect on us both spiritually and academically.

To get an idea of what this man is about I will share with you what he wrote in the V.C.H.S. yearbook of 1989.

Dear Grads: Education means "to lead out of". You may ask, "From where am I being led? " "Where am I being led to?" And who or what is leading me?" Education is a lifelong endeavor which should free you from the captivity of ignorance, helplessness, fear, selfishness, prejudice, and hopelessness.

Although the pathways are many none can escape the encounter with self, society and ultimately with God. As your journey continues may you walk in the ways of the One who calls you out of darkness into his marvelous Light.

Lawrence Farley

Mr. Farley introduced himself to us as the school's guidance councilor. I instantly just adored this man and just hoped I would soon be joining this school. I remember him chatting with both Sam and I before we all adjourned back out into the corridor to meet with my mother. Larry introduced himself to my mother Julie and said to her what special daughters she had and that she should be very proud. My mother replied, "I know they are and I am exceptionally proud of them both". I also remember meeting Mr. Descent for the first time that day as he walked up to us in the corridor. He had been in the room with Larry when Mr. Giguere had come in and asked Larry to join him in his office to meet Sam and I, so he knew we were from England and that Sam spoke beyond her years and of course took the opportunity to meet us both while we were in the corridor chatting. Phillip Descent was about five foot six with blonde hair that was thinning on top with a trimmed beard and moustache, he was stocky in build and he was wearing tinted glasses. Mr. Descent was very charming, he spoke to Sam and I like equals and asked us about England and how we were finding Canada so far. I remember him saying, "So you're the young ladies from the old country" and he had this quirky sense of humor about him where he would say things almost tongue in cheek and be smiling and laughing while he talked. We instantly liked him, not all the kids did though especially the trouble makers that he had pegged; they hated him for being on their case. Mr. Giguere said to Julie that he and Larry had a lot to discuss not just amongst themselves but with the entire faculty, that this was something that could not be entered into lightly and that he would be in touch. Things were looking hopeful.

To our guardians of V.C.H.S

(III)

The salvation of man is through love and in love

Victor E Frankl

Before we even started high school, we had made friends with some of the English children in the neighborhood, Nancy and Catherine. They had told us that there was a high school dance at V.C.H.S. at the end of September, to welcome all of the new students and start the new school year off. They invited us to the dance with them, even though we were not students of V.C.H.S. yet.

It was awesome. There are all these teenagers, and music blasting, colorful disco lights flashing around the hall, that you could see as soon as we came through the big main doors. Teenagers, making out with each other in the hallway and in various discrete corners, just off from the watchful eyes of the appointed guardians. Girls dancing together on the dance floor while the boys watched. The boys all congregated in designated corners of the room, depending on their year. Awkwardly they would stand too close to the edge of the dance floor, observing the girls dancing but unwilling to join in. When beckoned by a group of dancing girls to join them they would freeze with cold fear, looking like badly placed mannequins in a shop window that are in desperate need of rearranging, then begin to backup seemingly unaware of their friends they are backing into, which would insight a banter of pushing and pulling from the group, ignoring the girls until emotions had calmed crisis avoided and the boys could return to looking on like it was a spectator sport. Boys never seemed to want to dance with the girls throughout all of our high school years, unless it was a slow dance and a possibility of a kiss and a grope at the end of it.

It was the best thing I'd ever been to. I handed my coat over to the cloak room girl and she in return gave me a ticket with the number sixty-nine on it. Now bearing in mind I was twelve and this meant nothing to me, so I just put it in my pocket and moved on into the hall where all the action was going on. Not long after we got there with Nancy and Catherine, we met another girl called Kim, in the girl's washrooms. It turns out that this is where the real party is going on, girls sneaking booze, smoking cigarettes and using the mirrors to put on more make-up while talking about boys, sex and gossiping about the most resent school dramas that had befallen some poor child. This is where you really want to be. All the cool girls hang out here, doing all the cool things.

Kim seemed like she was years older than us and so mature. She was the coolest, dressed up just like Madonna, with white laced fingerless gloves on, high-heels and the dress looked like she had borrowed it straight out of Madonna's wardrobe and her make-up, the red lipstick, blue eye-shadow and the thick black eyeliner. Kim had shoulder length afro Caribbean hair, light coffee colored skin and dark brown eyes. Her father Bob is African-Canadian born and raised in Quebec. Her mother Rita is of European decent also born and raised in Quebec and saw herself to be a true bilingual. She would start a sentence in English and finish it in French. Kim was wearing an outfit that in reality was too old for her years because she was only twelve; her thirteenth birthday wasn't until that November. The way she walked around that high school dance like she was the V.I.P. guest invited to the party and boys were looking at her like she was the one they wanted to know. She knew how to act and how to talk and she was introducing Sam and me to everyone and informing us on who was who and what was what.

The school dance ended with the song *Stairway to Heaven*. Apparently this was their signature song which told you that the dance was over, no other song would be played after that. All the girls and boys would quickly find either the person they wanted to dance with all night or just anyone that was willing to dance with them because it was the last song and that is all your getting. It was the best night of our lives so far. We felt like we had made it. All we needed now was to be allowed in the school.

By the end of the night we had to queue up for our coats. To make the queue move faster there were four kids taking tickets and handing back coats, not just the one girl that was there at the beginning of the night. We had gotten in the queue midway with Kim and we were still chatting to all these new friends we had made when I got to the front of the queue and took that ticket out of my pocket and handed it over to the teenage boy behind the counter in the cloak room. He looks at the ticket and shouts out. "Number sixty-nine, soixante-neuf we have ourselves a winner".

All the kids there in the queue and the ones that were cleaning up after the dance start to cheer, clap and wolf whistle at me. I had no idea what was going on, but I was very embarrassed. I went as red as a beetroot.

Kim tries to reassure me by saying. "it's a sexual thing don't worry about it."

I had no idea what she meant but that wasn't very reassuring. I just wanted to curl up in a ball and have the floor open up and swallow me whole. Welcome to high school there was more of that to come for sure.

Mr. Giguere and Mr. Farley spent a lot of time reading Bill 101 and all points of law that related to education in the hope that they could find a loophole so that they could take me into the school legally. They were hoping for an exemption clause that would allow children with learning difficulties to attend English schooling. They tried to go about it legally first by applying for an exemption in the law, because of my learning difficulties. We were declined because there was no exemption and there was to be no exceptions to the law. Of course all of this took time and school had already started for all the other students and once more Sam and I were left on the side lines wondering what was going to happen next. Mr. Giguere and Mr. Farley decided that it was time to discuss this issue with the entire school faculty.

A meeting had been called by Mr. Giguere for the entire school faculty, including the secretaries. This was not able to be done until all of the teachers had come back off holiday to start the new school year during which time they had been trying to get us in the school legally. It was now late in October and Mr. Giguere and Larry explained to them the situation with Sam and me. How I needed a lot of support because of my learning difficulties and that I had not yet been able to grasp English or French like a normal child would have by now and that I needed a lot of help. From meeting me they could see that I would probably not survive what I was going through, if I was left to go back to French primary school on my own. They explained that they felt that I did need to be kept with my sister for now until I had progressed more with both my English and French.

From what I know, Mr. Giguere did put his point across that his meeting with Sam made him feel like he had a duty to help us. That he felt that she was a unique child that had an emotional intelligence beyond most adults, and was most probably a child genius. Mr. Giguere was a man that believed in academic excellence and saw in Sam something worth fighting for and I believe he wanted to be a part of that.

What I do know is they had to vote on it. They all had to be in it together or they all had to be out. Because all it would take is one phone call and it would be over for all involved. What was being asked of them was beyond their duty as teachers and could not be entered into lightly. They needed to go home and think about it and discuss it with their husbands and wives because if ever it was to be discovered potentially they could lose their jobs, their careers and their liberty. It was a decision they needed to sleep on and take the time they needed to make a decision they could live with. They weren't just teachers some were mothers and fathers. They had greater responsibilities outside of these academic walls. These were men and women that would have to stand before a judge and their peers in a court of law and say why they broke the law to protect a child; with the knowledge that those judging them, may be Separatist's and members or supporters of the Parti Québécois. They may not have been inclined to help this learning disabled child.

To this day, I believe something extraordinary took place because some of those staff members were Separatists and Parti Québécois supporters. This meant that they had to battle within themselves, their politics and the rule of Law and the needs of a child. It was a unanimous vote of yes. They were all in it together, this pact bonded these teachers and faculty. Apparently from what I was told years later they all agreed whole heartedly and I have asked Rev. Lawrence Farley how that was possible, considering we had teachers of many different backgrounds, some being in favor of Bill 101 and Parti Québécois, making a potential life changing decision not just for me but for them, if it was ever discovered. In truth they were a beautiful and varied mixture of exceptionally well educated teachers and staff from different religious backgrounds, ethnic groups and political persuasions.

Rev. Farley said to me "it was a miracle they were all on board to help you both because despite their differences and disagreements they may of had with each other when it came down to children they were very dedicated to educating and caring for them. The needs of the child prevailed."

Mr. Giguere was asked the same questions years later by Sam as to why they all chose to do this for us and he said, "It was done for humanitarian reasons. We knew we were breaking the law but the child needed us. You know, you were the first but you were not the last. Once we had done it for you, we thought well we might as well, so we took on a few more."

Giguere had strength of character that came from deep within him. He was the man that steered the ship with intelligence and reason. Once he had made a decision it was final. Giguere has a charm and charisma about him that is adored by all who know him. There are characteristics that come out in the way he handles situations and people that make him unique and formidable.

Rev. Farley told me a story about him many years later that sums up the man we all love. A father of one of the students at V.C. came in and began to rant and rave at Mr. Giguere in his office. At the end of his rant, he said to Giguere, "You teachers have not lived; here you are stuck in this school in this office day in, day out. You have not experienced this world. I have been half way around the world and know what I'm talking about".

Mr. Giguere's response to this man was, "Good for you, I have been all around the world and I have two doors in this office and you can use either of them to leave."

With all of my heart I thank you, you saved my life, you protected me, you nurtured me, you taught me everything I needed to know about the world before I was to journey out on my own. You were my guardians and like parents to me and for that, I love you all. V.C.H.S was not just any school; it was the best school that any child could have gone to. We are a family that is forever bonded. As I write this I realise that I am speaking out of turn because not all children could go there, for my brothers and sisters of Quebec that never had the opportunity because of Bill 101, I apologies with humility.

It was late October before they finally took us into the school. I was so excited to be starting high school because I already had this image in my mind of what it would be like from television shows. To be surrounded by all these teenagers and that I was one of them. It was great. I was growing up. I felt so much more mature. We had already made so many friends thanks to Nancy and Catherine and now we had Kim, who became our best friend since the night of the dance. Kim had invited us over for dinner the following week to meet her family. It was clear that she was going to be a big influence on us throughout our high school years. Sam was happy because we had another great bus driver once again. His name was Serge. His English wasn't very good but that was fine because Sam could now speak French and I would do my best to muddle through, by saying things like, ça va and salut, oui and non. He was a very jolly man of about five foot five, over weight with thick greasy dark brown hair, brown eyes and crooked teeth that could have done with a dentist bless him, but he was a lovely man. As soon as he saw us at the bus stop as he opened the school bus doors, he shouts out, "Les deux gemelle nes pas?"(Twins, no?)

Sam responds with her best charming smile, "Bien oui, les deux gemelle, salut, ça va?" (Yes we are twins, hi and how are you?)

That was it; he loved us we were his deux gemelle Anglais. By the end of the week Sam's charm had this man picking us up outside the front of our house. We now had our own bus stop, it was called "chez nous" that is what the bus driver called it, "your house". Every day that man would stop outside our house honking his horn, calling us to get on the bus, because Sam was not a morning person and was always late, the bus driver would call, "allez, allez, les deux gemelle. Vite, vite, c'est tres tart". (come, come the twins, quick, quick it's late; which I know doesn't translate too well) and Sam would reply, "juste deux minute, je fais mes cheveaux, s'il vous plait"(just two minutes, I'm doing my hair please). And if it wasn't Sam calling to the bus driver for more time to get ready, it was me calling out of the window of our bedroom for more time for Sam and in French, no less. But this man adored Sam so he would wait for her. He used to have to honk his horn many times for her to hurry up but he was loyal and adored his deux gemelle anglais.

I remember the first week at V.C. was exciting and a little scary. The grounds were so big and I had no sense of direction and would easily become lost. Kim took Sam and me on a tour of the campus one lunch time by the end of the first week. For a twelve year old kid it seemed massive and overwhelming, especially the French side. It was over twice the size of our side of the campus. It was so quiet, like there were no students or staff there. Sam asked Kim why that was. Kim explained to us that the French and English students were kept apart by keeping us out of sync by one hour. We were puzzled by this.

"What do you mean by one hour?" Sam asked Kim.

Kim stopped walking and turned to us to explain. "The French and English are kept apart by keeping us in different time zones. We start school at just gone eight o'clock and they start exactly one hour later. That way we are all kept apart from each other by a time difference. It stops any fighting and conflict. Things might not be so bad now but just a few years back the fighting got so bad between the French and English we had curfews imposed in Montreal. They needed to do something to keep the kids from killing each other. But also, it allows us to use all the same facilities like the school busses, the auditorium, canteen, swimming pool and gym. Clever really when you think about it, it serves a dual purpose."

Sam responds, "I guess it is but it also means the students have nothing to do with each other. They are here on the same campus and yet they don't even know each other. It keeps us separated not allowing us the chance to develop friendships. Language is not enough to keep us apart so now we have time to keep us separated."

Kim, "I never thought of it that way, because we still have some friends that are French, we just hang-out with them when they get back from school and at weekends.

Sam then asks Kim. "So do they use the same bus routes to pick-up the French kids just an hour later and is it the same bus drivers?"

"Yeh, why?"

"Just wondering"

Telling Sam she could get a bus into school one hour later with her already well trained bus driver was like all her Christmases coming together. From now on, if Sam wanted a lay-in she would. This time zone separation was going to serve her dual purpose. She got to make loads of new friends on what Sam would now call "the later bus" with the French kids in our neighborhood from the other side of the campus and she got to sleep-in once in a while. Two things my sister loved, making new friends and sleeping-in. It was the best news she heard all year and we'd only just got here.

Sam and I were all of about four foot eight inches. We were tiny little things, with our hair tied back into pony tails and me with my little finger curl I had in the front of my forehead which was the only way anyone could tell us apart by just looking at us, we were that identical. Even the secretaries would say to me, "whatever you do, don't you get rid of your curl because it is the only way we will ever be able to tell you two apart". There we were, standing in the hallway next to my sister's locker, and our new best friend Kim with us chatting and suddenly these big tall seriously handsome men that looked about twenty one to me but in reality were sixteen, seventeen, scooped Sam and me up off our feet, they had one each and were throwing us up in the air and catching us and cuddling us like we were their dolls to play with. We didn't even really know these men. We had only seen them in the hallway about twice and it was our first few days here.

They were saying. "You are so cute you're like our little dolls or baby girls."

I could not believe it Sam and I were shouting at them to put us down and they weren't taking any notice. They were big and strong, they looked and smelt great, their Ralph Lauren cologne and sweaters to match; it was so devastating to us both.

Sam said to them while they were still cuddling us. "We're not your bloody dolls, were teenage girls now put us down".

They just laughed at us like they loved their babies even more for being able to talk and asked us to say something else.

"Sam replied. "You can bugger off".

They loved it, "say it again we love your accents"

"Ok, bugger off. In fact you can piss off and put us down"

Sam and I were not amused. Not only were we painfully aware that our class mates were watching but most of the school were present, including some of the teachers and they were all laughing. Everybody in the school is watching us being treated like this. They were even kissing us on the cheeks like we were their little babies. I was devastated just please God make it stop I've only just got here and I'm losing all hope of any street credibility in this new school. There was me hoping that I could reinvent myself and be respected and thought of as cool. Well we were liked alright, these guys loved us, just too much and not in the way any young girl wants to be loved. These older boys did this for the entire year. They just loved us, we were their little sisters. They found playing with us irresistible because to them we were nothing more than cute little dolls. They were immune to any form of retort we threw back, to get them to stop. Even when Sam and I would on occasion kick them in the shins or balls for going too far in smothering us with kisses and tossing us from one to the other. Being thrown in the air would scare us and make us scream, which we felt was not good for our street-credibility. Even the older girls loved us. We were always invited to sit at the back of the bus with them and they would chat to us and ask if they could play with our hair. It was really great, because we were known by them all. Our popularity with the older children was firstly due to the novelty of us being tiny identical twins from England. But it became more than that, once the novelty wore off, they had grown very fond of us, just for our own individual characters.

They genuinely adored us and to be honest, it did us a world of good to be that loved by these older children. By the end of the year when those students left for college and the real world, Sam and I cried and we did hug and kiss them good bye, because we had bonded with them, as if they were our older siblings, they looked after us and helped us settle into high school. We were going to miss them very much and we were aware that thanks to them we had become very popular students which filled us with self confidence and a sense of belonging even though we knew that we were there illegally.

Our first year of high school had its ups and downs. It wasn't all smooth sailing even though we had a lot of the grade elevens students taking us under their wings. I remember I couldn't have a locker next to Sam's because they were already all taken, so I was put next to an older boy from secondary three, who had failed a couple of times and happened to be the size of a house, but his physique was more fat than muscle. He had bad teeth and ugly strawberry blond hair, a freckled face and chubby fat hands. He was horrible and very much a bully.

The first week there my dad was supposed to get Sam and I locks for our lockers but had forgotten, so this boy stole my lunch out of my locker and ate it in front of me, while denying all knowledge. I could not believe it. I went to my locker at lunch time and there he was stood right there, eating my baloney sandwich, my dad had made for me the night before, with my lunch bag in his fat cubby hand. I opened my locker and my lunch was gone, he had it in his hands. I closed my locker and said to him, "did you just nick my lunch, is that my sandwich?" He stared right in my eyes, with his beady little ugly mishmash of light green and blue eyes and said, "Nope". The fat git, I was hoping he would just choke on it. I had no lunch and no money to get anything so Sam had to share hers with me. The next day on the Friday Sam had to put my lunch in her locker with hers so that he wouldn't get his big cubby hands on it and my dad had promised to stop by the local Wal-Mart on the way home from work and get us locks.

I remember this boy picked me up in front of my locker because he asked me where my lunch was today and I said that I had hidden it from him and I called him a fat git. He just lifted me up above his head and told me that if I didn't behave myself he would snap me in half. This was because I was standing up for myself. I wouldn't take being pushed around by him. He wasn't like the other kids here that seemed to like and adore Sam and me, he was rotten. Sam had turned up to meet me at my locker with Kim, Karen and most of the girls from our class and she was shouting at me not to do anything. Which to a guy that size was probably confusing. Sam was saying, "Don't you dare, the deal was no fighting remember you can't". She was referring to the deal made with Mr. Giguere and Mr. Farley that we were to be on our best behavior.

In our other two schools Sam and I had developed a reputation for fighting; even bullies had a hard time with us. So the deal was if we were given the chance to come to this school the fighting was to stop. Defending ourselves and fighting seemed to become a way of life for us. This was because of issues we faced in England, then the conflict we had to deal with in Greenfield Park and in Point-Claire where we had a continuous barrage of disagreements with children that hated us purely because we were from England. Although we were very small we had become at times like little pit-bulls. As the saying goes, "it's not the size of the dog in the fight; it's the size of the fight in the dog that counts". I guess it had an effect on our behavior and left us with this bad reputation, which to be fair was unjust because in truth we were only defending ourselves. I didn't touch this boy my word meant more to me than being threatened by a Neanderthal like him. I did notice that before the end of that year he had left anyway.

There was unfortunately one incident that year that I regret, in the spring of '85. It was Karen's thirteenth birthday and that morning the boys from our year seven had brought in eggs to egg her with. Before classes started in the morning we would all wait in the hall and just sit on the few lunch tables left out for us. There was a table for each year and the students always stuck to the same tables; there was never any changing around table to table, say from year seven to year nine and the area around that table belonged solely to that year. This of course is human nature, we all stick in our groups, we're all territorial and we don't like change. Karen was using Sam and me as shields against the boys egging her, and as girls do, we were laughing and squealing, well Karen was anyway. But what Karen was doing to get out of the way of the boys was dragging Sam and me backwards into the grade eight area of the lunch tables.

Now as Karen was doing this while squealing, screaming and pulling on Sam and me the boys from grade eight were trying to tell us to get back over to our side; because we were not allowed over their side. To be honest we didn't noticed them or what they were saying so finally when Karen had let go of us, one boy called Stephan from grade eight who had gotten annoyed with us for not listening went to slap me. It was only then I became aware of him or his friends, unfortunately for him, I blocked his slap and smacked him straight in the face and ended up towering over him saying, if he tried to hit me again I was going to put him through a wall.

This was not the best way to handle the situation; the whole school had seen it and was laughing at him. I then became aware of what I had done, but it was too late the boy's ego was destroyed. I felt regret but regret is impotent in the sense that it cannot undo what you have done. This boy was humiliated and to be honest, I felt so sorry for him at the time. It was pure reaction on my part, there had been no thought involved. His friends were not going to let it drop though, from that day on they started bullying Sam and me and we were not girls that took well to being bullied, we would fight back. This went on for almost a month it got to a point that all of us involved got called into Mr. Giguere's office. I was gutted (devastated) that I had let them down. I had broken my promise. We shouldn't even be in this school and I've made a mess of things. Mr. Giguere told us that it had been brought to his attention by almost every teacher and even the prefects that Sam and I were being bullied and that there was fighting going on in the hallways. He asked us all what it was about. The boys answer to this was, "they started it and we're finishing it". Which for teenage boys was a fair answer but it did not explain what had happened to cause this rivalry. Then Sam stepped up and explained what had happened to cause this situation and told him the whole truth in front of the boys. Mr. Giguere asked for this boy Stephan that I had smacked, to come down to the office and we all waited in Giguere's office until Stephen was brought in. Stephen was asked his side of things which was pretty much the same as ours but from his point of view.

Mr. Giguere had an amazing way of dealing with incidents like this and resolving them, because of the way he would talk to the students. He acknowledged the boys point of view of the situation by saying, "Ok, your friend has been humiliated not just by a girl but a younger smaller girl in front of the whole school, and you are loyal friends that want this girl to pay for humiliating your friend and I can understand that." He then turned to me and said, "What you did Justine was a reaction to being hit, you didn't think you just reacted. Ok so given the chance again would you have done it?" My response to him was, no. Mr. Giguere then said to me would you like to apologies to Stephan and I replied, "Yes, I am really sorry, given the chance again I would not have done that to you, I am sorry." Stephen accepted my apology and the other boys were told that there was to be no more bullying of us and we in turn were to not start any more fights. We all agreed and we're sent on our way and life did go back to normal for us.

That summer a new girl turned up in our neighborhood called Annick. Her parents bought a house across the road from us they were a French family that spoke English with a strong French accent. From the first time I met them they would try to teach me French, they would only speak to me in English if they lost me, and then they would revert back to their native tongue. They were adamant that it was the only way for me to learn. They would not give in and speak English to me. Most of the time I was clueless, struggling through with flushes of embarrassment, my inability to annunciate words would have me tongue tied and stuttering like a feeble fool. At times they would laugh at my mistakes, malapropisms most likely considering how much I would bring them to tears. Yet they made it clear that I was not to let that stop me and I was not to give up. My progress was so frustratingly slow. I made tortoises look lightening fast. Shortly after they had moved to the area, Annick's father Sebastien asked us, "how is it that you are able to attend an English high school? But you are from England, non?" My sister tried to tell him that we managed to fit loophole criteria and deflected the question by asking him about his job. Later that evening after spending most of the day with Annick walking all over Pincourt, introducing her to everyone we knew and going to the local mall, we came home to find Sebastien in our kitchen, with our parents talking. Sam decided to ease drop on what was being said. She came back a little while later to tell me that he had come around to find out how Julie and François had managed to get their daughters into an English school and he wanted the same for his daughter. I said to Sam, "why does he want his daughter to be educated in English? He's French and he told me French is the best language in the world."

Sam replied, "He might think that but he wants his daughter to have the same life opportunities as us and she probably won't get that if she stays in a French school. He wants his daughter to be able to attend an English college and university of her choosing to give her the best prospects."

I sat there on the window sill soaking up the heat from the sun before it faded into the night, just puzzled then said to Sam, "Why would the French stop their own children from having the best, it doesn't make sense?"

Sam sighed and said, "It's what I have said before, Bill 101 is revenge not equality they're hurting their own children."

How was it that these politicians of Quebec and Canada could not see what they were ultimately doing to their own children? Hate had a lot to answer for. Could there ever be a time in Quebec when language could be liberated and children of Quebec united in their education, making them truly bilingual, giving all children the same life opportunities.

When the second year came around Annick had somehow managed to enroll in our high school. That chat Sebastien had with our parents was obviously fruitful.

I was still in the same class with Sam; but because of my moods that were precipitated by my learning difficulties, that I was trying to hide from my teachers and peers, I had become volatile and even violent and I was taking it out on Samantha. This was not new to Sam. She had suffered this before from me in our previous school. The teachers had picked up on this and had made some comments about it in the staff room. Mr. Farley was then made aware of us being in the same class together this year and was surprised because we were supposed to have been separated by his and Mr. Giguere's request. What had transpired was because we were not in the school system due to our illegal status; the secretaries had to add Samantha and me to rotas separately after the legitimate rotas and documents have been made for the students and classes. There had been a mix up and I had been put in the advanced class with Samantha by mistake. What should have happened was that I was supposed to be kept in the lower class. Then they could have confronted me with my illiteracy issues and therefore helped me. It would have allowed Sam a chance to thrive without me clinging to her. That was the plan. They explained to me that I was supposed to be in the other class, not with Sam. I was devastated I begged them not to take me away from her. I even got my mom to request the same so I could remain in that class. Considering they were the more advanced group I actually liked this group better. I found I had more in common with them, they were intelligent like Sam. Most of the students enjoyed learning and could hold a good argument, debating in class on subject matters using empirical evidence and quotes from well versed authors. In some ways it gave me more to feed on academically, even though I was still sinking. Call it an accident or fate but I was able to get away with another year of hiding behind my twin.

In reflection maybe it was intervention because I don't think I was emotionally ready to handle coming out of the illiteracy closet nor was I mature enough as an individual to climb such a great mountain yet; because in truth it takes great courage and strength to perform such an act.

My English teacher, Mr. Decent pulled me aside one day after class and he posed a question to me that years later I have reflected on with a better understanding of what he was truly saying to me. "Justine, have you noticed that you are drawn towards the more academic students here despite your learning difficulties, you may have. Even though you were supposed to be in the other group this year, have you noticed that the students that you want to associate with are the ones that can teach you the most? You know there are more than just the traditional ways of learning in this world. I think that you are finding your own way of taking this world in around you. There are no accidents; I believe you deserve to be here just as much as anyone else. You have found your own way of learning, through others like your peers. "

Sam and I would pop in during break time to see Larry Farley, we, like many students would polarize towards him. He was on reflection our spiritual guide as well as our academic guidance councilor. We would spend the time discussing and debating the meaning of life our fellow beings and of course God and the words of Jesus. I enjoyed the allegories he would tells us. We would leave thinking about these morally infused colorful tales from a world that once was filled with disciples, prophets, and the son of God. A world that is thousands of years past and I would find myself wondering will there ever be another time like that once more. We would also share our day to day worries and woes with Larry. He was a man that could talk to all on every level. And his wife Susan made the best muffins which Larry loved to share with us all. Larry would come and find us at lunch break and tempt us girls that were trying to starve ourselves to stay skinny, with his wife's muffins. He knew there was no way we could resist her baking. Some of the girls in our group had become very concerned about getting fat; in fact it had become an obsession. It had influenced me on how I perceived my own body shape to the point where I was no longer eating lunch or breakfast. I gave up on the starvation diet in the end. I was sick of being famished. The hunger pains alone were enough to put me of dieting for life. My poor stomach would be screaming out for food, anything to fill such a hungry hole; making desperate, obnoxious loud noises during class; the starvation dragging out the school days, leaving me shaken and desperate for sustenance. It just left me miserable and weak. I loved food, besides I don't think I was any bigger for eating three meals a day or for that matter, for eating like a pig, which I had always done. I was just growing up and my body was changing.

This second year just flew by and we were very happy here with all of our school mates. We were a very close bunch of kids. Sam was still doing most of my work for me including tests, which was a burden for her and it was a shame because of what the teachers at Saint Jude's had achieved, in our first two years of school over here had been undone, by my year spent in the French school. It had just caused too much of a gap I guess in my education and caused arrested development academically, psychologically and emotionally. I was once again, completely leaning on Sam without even giving these teachers a chance. I just automatically reverted back to my old self and hid behind my twin. In defense of my teachers they were aware that I was dyslexic and had some form of speech delay and they were very supportive for the most part but I was out of my comfort zone. I felt like I was sinking and had no confidence at all, so leaning on Sam to do my home work and tests felt at the time like my only chance of surviving high school. What Sam would do is give me low grade C homework and tests so as to not arouse suspicion and she would even mimic my style of dyslexic writing, because to be fair there were times she could not be there for me and I would be left to muddle through on my own with what skills I had. With my own work I would usually end up with sixty percent or less.

By the end of the second year I had noticed Sam was trying to pull away from me more and at times I was left to fend for myself. Sometimes I just wouldn't do my home work, which lead me to end up in summer school, by the end of my second year for French and Math. Which, I had to do on my own without Sam. I loved math but for some unknown reason I had failed it this year and so ended up having to take summer school with Mr. Choi. To say not much got past this man was like saying that the K.G.B. was a little bit secretive. He had me sussed out in all of five minutes on the first day of his class, which was the first of many that summer with him. Looking back I think he had sown the seeds in me of taking the steps to changing my life and giving me the courage to do what needed to be done. He got me loving math again and I was good at it once more. I was getting 88% or higher on my work and tests it made me feel good about something again, like Mrs. Meehan and Mr. Hastings had made me feel, back in my first school in Quebec. Mr. Choi could see right through me and yet he made me feel safe. This was also the summer that Larry Farley became ordained in the Catholic Church and became Rev. Farley he also took back his Christian name of Lawrence instead of us all calling him Larry. I guess there had been a few seeds sewn that summer.

There was a down side to summer school too, for one, you did not get to hang out with your friends all day like everyone else and when your friends went off playing and swimming in their pools you were stuck at summer school in an uncomfortably hot and humid classroom, working hard to pass. And two, I also got locked in a locker for over an hour until Mr. Descent found me and let me out. Summer school always had the best kind of students in it, you know the ones you actually spent the entire year avoiding because they were nothing but trouble and going nowhere and if you weren't careful could take you with them. Stupid me, was standing next to an open locker when one of the older boys who was waiting in the hall with us for French class said to me "you know you're so small I bet you would fit right in that locker." Then before I had a chance to get out of the way he just pushed me in and closed the door and I was locked in, joy for me! I felt like a right idiot for getting locked in a locker. It wasn't even my locker. I was just stuck in there quietly calling out, "can someone let me out please? Anyone it's not funny anymore, please just let me out." Then Descent opens up the locker and says, "Need some help?" with that dry sense of humor of his. That incident made me way past late for French class and I needed that like a hole in the head. My French teacher was not impressed with me. I muddled through

French in summer school and passed, to this day I don't know how. What I can tell you is I did try my best without Sam's help for the most part.

By secondary three my understanding of French was getting there. I still couldn't speak it sufficiently, I hadn't a clue how to write it, but I was muddling by with the rest of the kids with what I had. They would at times speak both French and English to me and probably on a subconscious level my peers would take a conversation through in French until they could see they were losing me and then just half way through their sentences they would switch to English. This would also just happen because people that were bilingual would also naturally do this and unless I asked them to switch back to French they would continue the rest of the conversation in English. But you know it is not always the language you don't get sometimes it's the lack of life experience that you may be missing to understand your peers.

We were in Home Economics class all of us girls one afternoon and Christy was telling us all jokes while we were sewing our aprons that we needed to make for our assignment. I remember our home economics teacher Madame Palmieri was standing close to our two tables chatting and having a laugh with us girls. Christy decided to tell us a joke in French that her friend had told her the night before and she thought it was the funniest French joke she had ever heard. Christy says, "Pourquoi l'homme français est-il mort sur son soixante-dixieme anniversaire? C'est parce qu'il avait trop des soixante-neuf. (Why did the French man die on his seventieth birthday? It's because he had too much of the sixty-nine.) Everybody in class including Madame Palmieri was in fits of laughter but me. I didn't get it any more than I did at the first school dance; there's that number again causing me embarrassment and I don't even know why.

So I said to Christy, "I don't get it." that was even more funny to the rest of the girls they were howling with laughter especially Madame Palmieri.

Christy then says, "Let me tell it you in English."

I quickly reply. "I understood every word of what you just said, I just don't get how a man dying on his birthday just because he had too much of his last year is funny?"

Ok now they were screaming with laughter, Christy had tears coming down her face some of the girls were even complaining that their faces were aching from all the laughter.

I shout out, "What is so funny?"

Christy starts to draw me stick men, Madame Palmieri is saying to her, "leave it, she doesn't get it, don't". But no, Christy wouldn't leave it and her reasoning to Madame Palmieri for the need to explain this to me was, "she is almost fifteen, it's time she got a clue," and continues to draw two stick people and to my shock and horror they made the number sixty-nine.

Due to my speech delay and lack of mastering the English language, I was prone to saying the wrong words at the wrong time. My malapropisms had become notorious in school. My family would call it Dusty's Dictionary. Why Dusty's Dictionary, well the Dusty story will come later. The best one that I can recall was when in biology class in ninth grade I announced, "Sir, I just can't understand these orgasms." Dean, one of my class mates quickly responded and asked me if it was the multiple orgasms I wasn't getting or was it just the one? Mr. Grinham threw him a filthy look and by this time I had somehow caused complete chaos in the classroom. Ignoring the hilarity that I seemed to have induced I continued with, "seriously I don't quite get the single cell orgasms". Now I should have been left even more embarrassed than the sixty-nine incident but I was so clueless that it really just went beyond me. I seemed to be the only student that was not laughing and my lack of knowledge on the subject seemed to be making the class fall deeper into hysterical laughter. Mr. Grinham said it was an organism, and that I had mispronounced it and that he would explain later the organism that is, not the orgasm. I went home that night and had to ask my parents, when they finished laughing hysterically, as well they told me I could look it up in a dictionary or get back to them in a few more years when they were ready to cope with that one. I decided to leave it for now and ask Kim later at the weekend, since she always knew everything about things of which I had no clue.

The weekend came round pretty quick and Sam and I went to spend it with Kim and her family. Sam stayed in the kitchen with Rita helping her fold laundry. I accompanied Kim to her room to chat while she got ready for our night out. I sat on the floor with my back against Kim's waterbed while watching

Kim put on her make-up in her full length mirror she had fixed to her bedroom wall. She would spend what seemed to me hours getting ready before we would go out for the evening. I would just sit there watching her make such an effort applying foundation, then blusher, followed by eye shadow, mascara, and lipstick. It was clearly an art.

"Kim, what's an orgasm?"

Kim is now applying her blusher and looking at me through the mirror. "Why do you ask Jay?"

Kim never really calls me Justine, it has always been Jay.

"Well it kind of came up in Biology class."

"I didn't know we were doing sex-Ed in Biology, and I didn't think they were covering the orgasm."

"They're not but it came up."

"It's when a woman screams during sex." Kim has stopped applying her blusher in the mirror and is just talking to me through the mirror.

I kind of screw my face up thinking about what she has just said. "That doesn't sound good it just sounds really painful."

"It starts off painful but it becomes pleasurable."

"I doubt that very much if they're screaming." Was my answer to that one.

Well it's more like a good scream; I read all about it in Jackie Collins' books. Kim then starts to imitate what she has gleamed from reading such works as *The Bitch* and *The Stud*. With her blusher brush in her hand whilst still facing the mirror Kim starts to scream.

"Oh God, Oh God, Oh yes, Yes, Yes, YES." Kim turns to look at me.

"It's more like that, it's not about pain."

Rita, comes flying through the door at that moment, as though she is to find her daughter in the act of something, of what I'm not sure.

Kim, just turns to look at her mother and says. "For Christ sakes mother, can't you knock?" While throwing Rita a filthy look of contempt, then continues to apply her blusher.

Rita responds by giving me the worst glare I have ever had from her, but I am as moved by her glare as I am by our subject matter so far. You would have thought I had just had to sit through an hour long lecture about the invention of typewriters told in a monotone voice by a man that was being tested for a cure for insomnia.

"Well that's just great. I have been asking Mr. Grinham about screaming bloody women having sex, when I thought I was asking him about the single celled thing we need to learn for our test next week. No bloody wonder the class was in an up roar, that's just magic."

Kim turns to look at me and bursts into laughter. "Trust you Jay, to mix up a God damn orgasm with an organism."

Greenfield Park 1981-1983

(IV)

"The test of the morality of a society is what it does for its children."

Dietrich Bonhoeffer

I was nine years old before I learnt the Alphabet and I finally managed that by listening to the other children in the play ground singing the ABC song from Sesame Street. I would ask my friends to sing it to me over and over again, and I would join in, it was pure repetition of sound and relating it back to the letters on the front of the classroom wall above the black board and by watching Sesame Street as often as possible until it finally sunk in. I would sing the ABC song to myself every day a hundred times a day "now I know my ABC's wont you come and play with me?" That was in the first school we went to in Quebec, in Greenfield Park; it was a Catholic English primary school. We should not have been in that school either, we were breaking the law then as well. Saint Jude was the name of the school and the principal was an Irish man in his fifties, with a hint of his Irish accent left over from his life before Canada. Mr. Burke was small in stature and slim not an ounce of fat on him with a full head of grey hair and he was a heavy smoker. I remember the cigarette stains on his fingers, but then everyone smoked back then. He had emigrated here when he was a child. He was of course bilingual, which back then always fascinated me when I heard someone speak English and then switch straight back to French, with such ease. I remember him telling us that he came over by boat with his family and that it took a long time, and I remember thinking I wonder if he came over on the Mayfair like so many over here say that their ancestors did. I was nine at the time and not the brightest of children. He sympathized with my mother's problem of having to be forced to put her children into French schooling.

We didn't start school there until November of 1981 because it was not until my mother came to enroll us in the local English school, St Jude that she discovered that we were not allowed by law to attend English schools. It was a great shock to us all. Well, all but Sam, she already knew.

Back in England when we went as a family to London to meet representatives from the engineering company that brought us over to Canada because my step-dad was an electronics engineer, a bloody good one too. They showed us all a video about Canada and Quebec; how life was so great over there and how people lived life to the full and what was available in the way of recreation like sugaring off, ice-skating, canoeing and skiing and how beautiful the country is. You know the kind of videos, you're like wow when can I move there, it's the best place on earth.

Sam and I had just turned nine that spring. Sam had been reading up on Canada and Quebec ever since my mom and Step-dad had announced that we were moving there. We had this mobile library that came round in our neighborhood every week and stopped on our street on Crawford Road in Sheffield. Sam had been requesting books on Canada and their history. I remember the librarian ladies didn't like us much and kept having to tell Sam that she was only allowed children's books of a certain age. Sam would argue with them about what she should be able to read should be up to her, and her capability to read and comprehend. This came about because Sam had been requesting books on World War Two and the Nazi regime. Sam was not your average child. She started off like me, slow, but at about eight years old her brain kicked-in and there was just no stopping her. Oh and could she answer back; she had an answer for everything. She would have adults in knots. To be honest the average adult didn't have much of a chance against her, if she started on them. She wore those ladies down in the end. She got all the books she wanted and then some. Sam had also watched a documentary on the BBC about Quebec. The documentary exposed the struggles that Quebec was going through at the time with the separatist movement of the Parti Québécois; the recent changes in the law, such as Bill 101. There had been an English trade commissioner kidnapped and a Canadian politician, Pierre LaPorte, killed recently relating to this conflict and that there had been rioting and curfews set because of this.

The books the librarians had found for Sam had some evidence to support this and that it had been going on since the late sixties if not earlier. I remember Sam having a list of questions she wanted to ask these representatives, that she had made before we left for London. She asked our parents if it was ok if she asked some questions. My parents said she could ask all the questions she wanted, if that would make her happy. So she did and the list was long. It was probably the first time I have ever watched an adult squirm and look so uncomfortable with my sister's questions. I guess it felt like an interrogation to this woman or maybe it was because they didn't want the truth coming out about Quebec. It would not be good for business if engineers didn't want to move their families there with all of that going on.

Can you imagine disclosing all of the troubles of Quebec to English men before inviting them over where your company is based and saying;

"The French are going to hate you. There is rioting going on in the streets and bombings have been happening in Montreal in the Anglophone areas and curfews have had to be enforced, people have been attacked and killed. You're not allowed to speak English in any shops and your children will be forced into French schools, no matter how far along their education is already. Oh and your wife won't be able to get a job over there until she is fluent in French. And on the license plates of every car in Quebec they have the words "je me souviens", which means, "I remember." Which is a warning to the

English, that what was done to them is not forgotten and never will be."

I remember this lady talking to us like we were children at first and telling us how wonderful Canada was, and Quebec of course. How we would have so much to do over there and how exciting it would be for us to experience a new culture and learn a new language and make new friends. Sam was saying to this woman that she and I had watched a documentary all about Quebec on T.V. Sam started telling her all that she had seen about the sugar shacks and the predominant French culture, and that she knew that the official language was French. Up until this point, this woman was enjoying talking to us and was agreeing with what Sam was saying. She was even complementing both François and Julie on what intelligent and knowledgeable children they had. I remember François smiling with a tremendous amount of pride and saying "well of course, I'm not raising idiots". Then Sam said to her, "do you mind if I ask you some questions?" The lady replied, "of course, ask whatever you want." I bet she never forgot this child.

The list came out of Sam's pocket. "Is it true that the separatist movement of the Parti Québécois want to become a separate country from Canada and that there is a law that prevents people from speaking English in Quebec called Bill 101 and is it true that we will be forced to go to French schools? And that people had been kidnapped and killed?"

The woman's jaw might as well have hit the floor. She didn't even know where to start in the denial. At that point the two men that had gone mostly unnoticed in the room moved forward and tried to distract Samantha from her own questions. While the woman began to talk to Julie and François about how embracing the French culture was towards other cultures and that there were a lot of English families that had settled in Quebec. She continued her response to Sam's damming questions with the offer that she would be more than willing to introduce them to these couples, that were very happy living in Quebec. Sam tried to readdress this woman by saying "you haven't answered any of my questions." The woman looked at Samantha and smiled a patronizing, mouth closed smile of dismissal. My mother then said to Samantha that's enough now" and gave Sam that evil glare that means, do not push it or I will kill you.

These questions, of course, were never answered. However, in the pursuit of balance and truth let me answer them now. In October of 1970 Pierre Laporte a Quebec politician was kidnapped and murdered, strangled to death by the FLQ (Le Front de Libération du Québec) they were the left wing nationalist and socialist group in Quebec; they also kidnapped James Cross, a British Trade Commissioner, but he was later released in exchange for the free passage to Cuba of five of the kidnappers. The FLQ were responsible for the bombing of the Montreal Stock Exchange in 1969. In 1970 Quebec was put under martial law under the War Measures Act by Pierre Trudeau, who was the Prime Minister at the time; a man who feared no one and was willing to do what was needed to bring back order to Quebec. During this crisis he was once asked by a reporter how far would he go, and his answer was, "Just watch me" and that just about sums him up. Pierre Trudeau was the man that could not be moved. He won his position hands down because of his strength of character. When he was at the Saint Jean-Baptiste Day parade in Quebec in 1968 separatists were rioting throwing rocks and bottles at the grandstand right at him but he just sat there and faced them all. This period in 1970 in Quebec's history is known as the October Crisis (La crise d'octobre) The Montreal metropolitan area was the worst affected by the bombings and rioting. The FLQ were responsible for over 95 bombs ranging from mailboxes in the affluent Anglophone areas to targeting city Hall and the Royal Canadian Mounted Police recruitment offices and railways. The FLQ called for the independence of Quebec from Canada and the Parti Québécois was also calling for this. They perceived the English Canadians to be oppressors and referred to them as the Anglo-Saxon imperialist. One of the members of the FLQ François Vallieres wrote a non-fiction book called *The White Niggers of America,* which depicts how a lot of the French feel about how they are being treated, perceived and used by the capitalistic Anglo world.

The hatred here ran deep and was affecting everybody. You could not have lived and breathed in Quebec, whether you were Anglophone or Francophone, you would have been affected by this in some way. And yes, Camille Laurin's Bill 101 prevented many children, even Canadian born, from going to their choice of school; this took effect from 1977 to the present day. Bill 101 affected everyone's rights to the freedom to choose which language they wanted to speak-in and read-in and therefore think-in. The Québécois license plates that have been referred to earlier have great irony about it. Even though it symbolizes the French Québécois issues with the English, the true origins of "Je me souviens" are, Je me souviens, que né sous le lys, je croîs sous la rose. (I remember that born under the lily I grow under the rose).

This was honored in the work of Eugène-Étienne Taché in 1883, an architect of the provincial Parliament building. He had the motto carved in stone below the coat of arms of Quebec which appears above the Parliament Building's main door. The meaning of these three simple words changed again when Thomas Chapais in 1895 in a speech given in the unveiling of a bronze statue honoring de Lévis, *"yes, we remember. We remember the past and its lessons, the past and its misfortunes, the past and its glories."* These words were the representative of the beauty and diversity of Quebec and its past. How could something so positive become something so bitter? In 1981 the year we moved over to Quebec was the year that FLQ members, Marc Carbonneau returned as the prodigal son from living in exile in France and Francis Simard was released from prison after being convicted for the murder of Pierre Laporte.

We had started to make friends in our new neighborhood in Greenfield Park with the children in the welfare apartments from behind our newly built apartments. Michael and Nadine were siblings and had just come over one day and introduced themselves to our mother. They said that they had heard that some girls from England had just moved here into one of the new apartments and they wanted to make friends with us. I remember my mother calling us saying, "twinnies, there are some children here that want to make friends with you". Michael was nine and Nadine was ten. They had dark olive skin, dark brown hair and brown eyes. They were bi-lingual children, their mother was an Allophone, Italian decent and their father was a Francophone, their family were all bi-lingual and most of their cousins went to English schools even though they were all half French and some of them were half Italian and half French. None of them would have considered themselves English Canadians.

One of the first things I had noticed about these children that had befriended us was that they were so friendly and kind which I was not really accustom to. My life experience so far with children that we had been raised with in Derbyshire and in Sheffield Yorkshire had been different. The children were harsher not as loving towards each other or as kind and they physically fought a lot more with both their siblings and each other, there was a more aggressive tone about them. Our own brother who is much older than Sam and I spent a lot of time telling us to piss-off and used mainly threatening behavior to keep us at a distance. His idea of playing with us was beating us up and giving us Indian burns for fun.

Michael and Nadine treated each other with kindness and respect. They had a close relationship that I had not really seen with brothers and sisters so much. They made quite the fuss over us too, which was great. They took Sam and me all over Greenfield Park introducing us to all of their extended family and friends which meant all of their first, second and third cousins. It was hard to keep track it seemed like these kids were related to half of Greenfield Park and were friends with the other half. They were great kids to hang out with. They told us all the local gossip and did a lot of translating for us in shops and any public place where we needed someone to speak French for us. They took Sam and me to all the parks and the local swimming pool they were wonderful at introducing us to our new environment. We were soon known by everyone in the neighborhood and we were starting to settle in. Being from England and identical twins made us a double novelty to them. They loved listening to our accents and hearing stories about what England was like. What Sam and I knew about life in England was fascinating to them and their friends. They went to Saint Jude School and so we were even more eager to go there to be with our new found friends.

Mr. Burke had spent some time putting off our mother and probably deliberating over whether to take Sam and me into his school illegally. We finally started in November of 1981 as I mentioned earlier it was both exciting for us and long overdue because we were going stir crazy in the apartment. It had been decided that Sam and I were to be put in the third class of grade four children so that they could see how we would handle it and get a base line for us and if need be move up from there. Apparently in Canada they had three classes for each year and the children were put into groups according to needs and ability so that each child got the best out of the education system, what a novel idea. So they put us in the class with the children that needed more support than the children in the other two groups. I loved this class. There were children just like me, who were also struggling. And Michael my new best friend was in the class with us and half of his cousins were here too, so we already had friends in class, it was great. Some were even more learning disabled than me. One boy called Eddy who also had learning difficulties used to pee and pooh himself which was great because I finally found someone who had more problems than me. I only peed myself and was getting much better with that now that I had moved to Canada, so things were looking up.

For the first time and probably the only time in my life I felt like I fit in. And when I mean fit in we were like the Breakfast Club of misfit kids. We had each other and no one teased us, not enough to be bothered about anyway. Looking back now I realise that it was an amazing school because it was a school that did its best to include all children and make every student feel important. Their ethos was a positive one of inclusion of all and not exclusion of those deemed less worthy. The teacher they gave me was the best teacher I had ever had and was ever going to have either. Her name was Mrs. Meehan and she was like another mom to us all. I remember the first time Sam and I were taken to her class, Mr. Hastings, Mr. Burke and our parents were there with us. We were taking a tour of the school when we got to the class we were going to be joining. Mr. Hastings went into the class and came out with

Mrs. Meehan in toe. She introduced herself to us and shook our hands and talked to us like we were special. She had this ability to make us all feel loved and important. She asked us if we would like to meet the class and spend a couple of hours with them, Sam and I said in unison "Yes please." My dad said he didn't mind picking us up later, so it was agreed we just got straight in there.

She addressed the class by saying, "these two young ladies are the ones I was telling you all about this morning, they are from England, they're twin sisters and they will be joining us".

I remember all the children sat at their desks looking at us.

Mrs. Meehan then says "would you like to say hello to Justine and Samantha."

The entire class shouts out, "Hello Justine and Samantha"

Sam and I say "hello" back.

For the first time in my life I felt special and wanted. Mrs. Meehan made me feel special and the children made me feel special. She then asked us to take a seat in the class so we headed to the only two empty seats that were in the centre row. Wow I had my own desk to sit at and I noticed that their blackboards were on the wall not on easels, which is where I usually sat. She spent the time to get to know Sam and I and what our strengths and weaknesses were. She soon found out that I could not read or write and that I didn't even know the alphabet. She was fine with me about it, she didn't punish me for it. She was shocked with the fact that the school in England hadn't taught me anything, but she wasn't angry with me, so I felt safe. We also had Mr. Hastings come in and help teach us too which was great. I loved him. He was the coolest teacher ever in the Universe. Mr. Hastings was of British decent, the name gives that one away. He was of medium height, stocky looking man with blond hair with a hint of warm strawberry tones in it, he had a trimmed back beard and light blue eyes. I was to find out later that the reason he kept a beard was because he had been in an accident of some sort and it had scarred his face so he kept the beard to hide the scares. He was a laid back soulful character and his style of language depicted that. He was a bachelor and he had spent time travelling the world when he was younger it was on his travels if I remember correctly that he acquired his scares. He loved teaching children and treated them like they were his friends and he knew all of their names. (Not pupils that must be assimilated into greater society, that must fear and obey him, like I had been used to in England).

He amazed me I had never met a teacher like him before. All the children loved him and like me thought he was the coolest and they would say that he was their friend. This man was the vice-principal of the school and the kids adored him. He would come in and help me with all sorts like math and the alphabet. I was a very slow learner but he had the patience of a saint. Mr. Hastings was also our History teacher and I loved history, it was my favorite subject because we got to learn about what life was like in the olden days. It was like going in a time machine and hanging out in the past with the Romans and the Saxons. We got to hear about battles and all sorts of cool stuff. When I look back now, I realise that it was Mr. Hastings that made it that exciting for us kids. He was very visual with his story telling he was the one that took us back in time; it was his time machine his colorful ways of teaching that made me love history. I became transfixed and wanted to learn more.

Sam and I had to go on a school bus for the very first time. We were going on a North American yellow and black school bus like you see in the movies, how exciting. And we had to stand and wait at a designated bus stop with our new school friends like Michael and his sister and a bunch of other kids too. I was so happy, I loved going to school for the first time in my life. I would stand there at the bus stop with my sister and friends with my schoolbag on my shoulder and my Flintstone lunch box in-hand that my dad had pact up for us the night before. My sister had a Snoopy lunch box which was good because it meant that we could not get them mixed up. I was just like any other child. The bus turns up; the driver opens the doors and the children one by one start to get in. Sam and I follow behind Michael and Nadine this bus driver is saying good morning to the kids in French (bonjour, ça va?) and to our amazement, it is a women bus driver with curly black hair and horn-rimmed glasses. She then sees Sam and me and she speaks a bit louder with excitement in her voice and she appears to be addressing us, so then Nadine responds for us. Sam and I are just stuck on the stairs in front of her with her talking in French to us and Nadine and Michael talking back to her, explaining that we are from England and that we don't speak French. She uses a word that I do remember and did need to learn over there quite fast and that is "deux gemelle" which means girl twins in French and from then on we were known as les Deux gemelle anglais (English twins). Sam and I used the only French we knew which was "ça va" and then grabbed a seat next to Michael and Nadine.

School buses are the best. You get to hang out with all these other kids on the bus on the way to school. We can tell each other jokes, sing, and mess-about and there are no adults here to tell you off. How cool is that? I loved taking the bus except when I had forgotten to go for a pee before leaving home or school. I was still having trouble remembering to go to the toilet. By the end of that year Sam and I had gotten to know the bus driver even though she could hardly speak a word of English and we could hardly speak a word of French. She loved us and would let us sit on her lap and drive the bus with her, she was great.

Our first day at school was the biggest cultural shock of all. We had our own lockers right outside the classroom, we had never had lockers before. When we got in class and sat down ready to start the day with all the other students coming in and individually saying, "Good morning Mrs. Meehan," we couldn't really grasp why they were all so friendly with her and she would respond to each child with love and kindness asking them how they were feeling today. She seemed really interested in every one of her students.

When we were all seated, then two older children knocked on the door and came in and stood in front of the class. Then we heard the intercom come on and Mr. Hastings and Mr. Burke were in turn addressing the entire school. How cool is that? They had an intercom system and were talking to everyone at the same time. You could tell by the tone in their voices and how they were addressing everyone that they loved this part of their job. They started with saying good morning to all of the students and faculty of Saint Jude and then began the morning prayers, which proceeded with asking everyone to stand for the national anthem so we all stood up and everyone in our class put there right hand on their chests and began to sing O Canada.

Oh Canada

Our home and native land!
True patriot love in all thy sons command.
With glowing hearts we see thee rise,
The True North strong and free!
From far and wide,
Oh Canada, we stand on guard for thee.
God keep our land glorious and free!
Oh Canada, we stand on guard for thee.
Oh Canada, we stand on guard for thee

Sam and I had never experience anything like this in our lives before and it felt great to belong to a country, with my hand on my heart I sang like a caged bird freed. Of course this is me were talking about I was using the wrong hand the whole time. I could not tell my left from my right; it was another six years before I got that one. Mr. Hastings then went on with any announcements that needed to be made and just when we thought it was over Mr. Hastings said over the intercom, "It's now time for the "Health Hustle, now remember follow your instructors." Sam looked at me and me at her like what is this, then music starts and everyone in class including Mrs. Meehan who was at the back of the class with us started to follow the two older kids in the front. "My Sherona" was blasting out of the intercom. I couldn't believe what I was hearing or seeing they were all dancing around doing the same choreographed moves to the music, everyone was doing this and they wanted Sam and me to join in. It was another world to me, a far cry from the misery of the British school we had come from. By the time we had finished I was in very high spirits thinking what are they going to do next? They did this every single day five days a week. I came to love it all, what a way to start your day off, praying to God, pledging to your country and dancing around your classroom.

Today was also the first time we were going to have lunch at school too. I could not wait because Michael said it was his favorite part of the day and you get to do trades, not that I knew what that was but it sounds fun. Lunch time came round and Sam and I just followed the other classmates to the lunch room and sat with Michael and Lee who was also going to become one of my best friends. Lee has a great sense of humor and we never stopped having fun. He was a lanky kid with auburn colored hair and hazel eyes and freckles and always wore a baseball cap. Sam and I sit down and start to tuck into lunch when we notice all the kids start swapping lunches and haggling with each other to try and bag large slices of pizza that some other kids have brought in. Pizza, how cool is this? It's like the stock exchange for kids and it was fast pacing too. It's so noisy and no teacher cares, they just let the trading go on uninhibited by any adults.

In fact when Mr. Hastings walks past and the kid that managed to trade up to pizza shouts out to Mr. Hastings, "I did it, I've bagged the pizza today". This boy then proceeded to take the biggest bite right out of his prized pizza. Mr.

Hastings response is, "that's great! Well done". Sam and I are just in complete awe of what we are seeing. Then the kids around us asked if we have anything to trade Sam replied, "I have some of my mom's homemade buns". One kid says "really, can I trade you my Twinki for one?" Sam says, "yeh sure". Then Lee asks me if he can trade his cake bar for my bun. I could not believe my luck. I thought we've got more of these buns at home, my mom's become a right proper Suzie home-maker since we got to Canada, she is always baking. I might be able to trade up to pizza if these kids like our mom's buns. Sure enough by the end of the year, I was trading up to pizza thanks to my mom's buns and I would ask for extra buns so that I could do even more trading. I was a very hungry kid; I could eat as much as two grown men. In fact my poor sister had to eat fast in our house like an inmate in prison. I was that bad with food. Sam would say if she didn't eat fast and keep an eye on her food she didn't eat, there was many a night she went hungry because she took her eye off her plate; that poor girl. And yes, I did feel bad but I couldn't help myself. I could eat for all of Canada and England put together and God knows where it went because I was tiny.

Sam was settling into the school quite well and getting very good grades. Almost every test she would get a hundred percent, except for the time she had one mistake on her spelling test. She was furious and accused Mrs. Meehan of making a mistake with her marking. I was shocked at how angry Samantha was. She told our teacher that it was her that could not spell the word colour and insisted that it had a letter "u" in the word, but Mrs. Meehan said, "I'm sorry Samantha but the word color does not have a "u" in it." Samantha was so insistent that she was correct about the spelling of the word that she felt that they both needed to go and see the principal Mr. Burke. They both went down to his office for Mr. Burke to make the final decision on how the word colour should be spelt and both returned victorious. It turned out that the U.K. way to spell the word has a "u" in it and the North American way does not. Samantha was awarded a mark of one hundred percent on her spelling test and the matter was settled.

Another occasion when Samantha and Mrs. Meehan had a cultural difference was when a boy in class was misbehaving. The teacher had asked this boy to stop misbehaving and the boy continued his outburst.

Samantha raised her hand, "Miss, are you going to hit him if he continues?"

Mrs. Meehan responds with a nurturing tone in her voice, "No Samantha, we don't hit children just because they behave badly."

Samantha then asks with curiosity, "Why don't you just hit him Miss?"

"Because it's against the law to hit children Samantha and it's not how we treat children here." With a sense of concern in her voice for what she is hearing from this child.

Samantha then retorts, "So, shall I hit him for you Miss?"

"No Samantha. Nobody hits anybody here, you can't smack him"

The boy has by now stopped to listen to what is being said and begins to calm down. I think he was a bit concerned that Sam might actually hit him.

Not long after Sam and I had started school in Saint Jude's Mrs. Meehan needed to leave the room for a minute, as soon as she left Sam jumps up on her desk and shouts out, "woo hoo... she has left the class, who hates Mrs..." Then looks around to see all the other kids looking at her like she is insane and Michael and Lee shout out to her, "What are you doing?" At this point I was climbing up on my desk to join her then realise that no one else is and quietly climb back down and sit. Sam was just standing on her desk like a complete boob, this was no *Dead Poets Society* moment, "oh captain my captain", I can tell you.

Sam says. "Don't you kids do this over here? You know, when the teacher leaves the room, you run wild, jump up and down on desks, scream and shout about how much you hate your teachers and principal and hate school, no, anyone?"

One boy, Chris says "we don't hate our teachers we like them and our principal. Why would we hate them?"

Michael then says to her. "Why would you act like that any way?"

Sam gets down off the desk and sits quietly. Good point why would we be used to acting like feral children when the teacher leaves the room. What had the English system done to turn children into this? Kids that hated their teachers so much and had absolutely no respect for them what so ever, all they really had from us was fear and the belief that we were worthless. Mrs. Meehan returned to her class unaware of the incident, thank God.

I started to notice that my mom and dad were settling in too. Dad at his job and my mom was happy with this beautiful brand new apartment with all the mod-cons like a dishwasher and cable T.V. with twenty four channels. We only had four channels in England and most of them switched off by a certain time. Some of the Canadian channels were French channels of course but to be fair, I think there were more English channels and there were all the American channels too, so in some ways it was like we had America living on our doorstep, they were just a channel away. I remember Good Morning America being on every week day and that became mine and Sam's favourite program because it was informative in telling you what was going on in the world. Good Morning America was really all we had to keep our brains occupied, while Sam and I were not yet at school, just stuck at home, day in day out, not even having our friends to play with because they were at school all day. That's the only thing I missed about going to school, was not being able to watch Good Morning America all the way through to the end of the show every morning.

It was a different story for Alex though, my older brother. He was fifteen and my mother could not get him into an English school, they would not touch him and he had refused to go to the French high school and so he just dropped out; no school no job and not much of a life for him. Looking back on this now as an adult, I realize that the lies told by the engineering company contributed to a lot of damage, they are not the main contributors but they did play their part. They knew that my step-farther François had a teenage step-son and step-daughters. We were all there together at the meeting, when they were telling us all about the great outdoor activities of Canada and how fantastic Quebec is. And, it is not like one of us there didn't ask some very poignant questions, about Bill 101, and how it would affect our education. However, it was also down to my parents because they did not do their homework. Their own lack of due diligence was of course the main contributing factor. They were blinded, by their desire for a better life out of England because in the late seventies and early eighties England had its fair share of problems too. With rioting in the streets and many of the unions striking, at times the country felt like it was on its knees. The working class hero's of Great Britain had had enough of the class system in England and being paid a pittance for a hard day's work and being subjected to poor working conditions, for those who could get a job, that is. Unemployment in Britain was at an all time high and the tension amongst the lower classes was rising, they also wanted to be treated better by the upper class system that was controlling their lives. So my parents took all that was told to them on face value because they wanted out of England and wanted better for themselves. My brother could have got his arse out of bed and made an effort to go to school and give it a chance, he did take advantage of the situation. He could have made the effort; he was after all an intelligent young man. My parents could have made him go to school and not tolerate his teenage attitude and defiance but that's not what happened.

We had our first Christmas here, which was fantastic it was of course to be the last Christmas we would believe in Santa Claus. I remember my parents got the neighbor, Eric from down stairs to dress up as Santa and do the whole, "ho, ho, ho", thing and put our large stockings filled with presents at the end of our beds. They even took Polaroid's, which is kind of what tipped us off with the whole Santa not really being Santa. Especially the one with my mom on Santa's knee, I don't think the real Santa would grab my mom's bum like that. Our first Christmas was also interesting because at school the kids would ask each other, "do you open your presents in the morning or after midnight?" I thought this was a strange thing to ask. It turned out, that what they really wanted to know was, is your family English, or are you in fact from French decent. The kids that said they opened their presents after midnight mass got a punch in the arm, and called French frogs, and were laughed at, which I found to be cruel and uncalled for. Why did children need to even go there? I didn't care when my friends opened up their presents, nor did I care if their families were really more French than English.

It was taking some time for me to realize that this school was nothing like what we had experienced before. You see it's easy to condition a child one particular way, but to then recondition, that can sometimes take a little longer. Like an elephant with a chain securely fastened around its leg, when it's just an infant, it learns that no matter how hard it tries to escape, it's not going to get out of that chain. So when it's finally learnt that lesson the ring-master can just put any old tattered rope around its leg and not even tie it to anything and that elephant's going nowhere. It's called classical conditioning. We had been at the new school only weeks as Christmas was approaching, when Mr. Burke and Mr. Hastings had announced over the intercom a Christmas card making competition. All the children in our class were very excited about this, Samantha included, but not me. I had seen it all before. As far as I was concerned, it was fixed and the children of the PTA Mums would be the sure winners. Sam went straight home to start her perfect idea for a card and expected me to fully cooperate with her, as per usual. Sam and I made everything together. We always made great partners in our arts and crafts experiments, from Wonder Woman outfits with matching bullet-proof bracelets to wooden furniture for our dolls. We even made a go-kart once but on its maiden voyage, down the top of Crawford Road (our old road back in Sheffield England) it fell apart, with bits abandoning ship before our very eyes. With the both of us sat on it. Our bums clenched as tight as our fists around the rope we were using to steer this beast, going even faster with less on the damn thing, until we finally crashed into our neighbors' wall. We had forgotten to put any brakes on it. We weren't allowed yet to use any nails or screws since we were only seven at the time and we thought rope would do. But I had had my fingers well and truly burnt in the old school, in England and was not about to ever try again. As far as I was concerned, that chain was made of steel and never coming off. Sam had this great idea, for a pop out Santa for our card. It was going to be the best card they had ever seen, with a great big jolly red Santa popping out saying "ho, ho, ho, Merry Christmas!" I didn't want her to put so much effort into it because I knew it would be a waste of time, we weren't going to win. So really what was the point? Our last Easter in Sheffield, our school had an Easter egg competition for the best decorated egg. Sam was determined to pull out all the stops for this one; we could not possibly lose. She decided we were going to make a farm-house, a spring awakening on the farm with all the animals, including the farmer and his wife. Made out of real eggs, hard boiled and hollowed eggs that we had blown the insides out of ourselves, which in itself is an art. There was a farm house made of cardboard and lollypop sticks, a barn for the animals, a pond made out of shinny tin foil and a fence made out of twigs. We had real grass in the fields and the sheep were covered in cotton wool. The detail that went into making this work of art not to mention the time and money, our spending money, was more than most children would do at 'A' level never mind at the grand old age of nine; we were just turning nine that Easter. The weight of it was something else. We had not considered how heavy this model of a spring farm life was going to be. It almost killed us carrying it down to school. It had a base made of thick cardboard that we had gotten from the lady that owned the corner shop down the road from us; along with all the glue, paper and other miscellaneous arts and crafts bits that Sam thought we needed to make this Easter masterpiece, including the eggs. And eggs cost a pretty penny, even back then. All the children began to follow us down to school, like we had become the pied pipers with this masterpiece in hand. Children were wowed by what we had made, and were asking so many questions about how we had crafted such a thing. I could hear in Sam's voice and the way she was explaining how we had gone about creating such a grand piece, that she was very proud of our work and the attention it was getting us. She thought we were sure winners. We brought it into the main hall and placed it onto a table, where Sam wrote our names on a card and our class year.

Later that day all the children that had entered the competition had to return to the hall and stand next to their work and be judged. Enter stage left the PTA, with the teachers' in-toe. There was only four other children competing in our group with Cadburys Easter egg boxes, coloured in with felt tip pen and crayon, cut into slightly different shapes, and you could tell that their PTA mothers had helped them with the finer details, like cutting and colouring. Let the judging begin and it did. I stood there next to my sister my head bowed low. Even with all the children around our table, saying how fantastic our farm was and what a great idea it was. I was ashamed and didn't like being here, with these teachers and PTA mothers. It was only the children that thought this; the adults barely looked at our work, that we had put our blood, sweat, and tears in. We had already been judged by them, and we had been found wanting a long time ago. We didn't even come third. That was it for me no more, not ever. I was done.

Now here we go again. Sam's got us putting far too much effort into something we can't win. So I said to her, "I'm not doing it. They're not having the best that we can do just to snub us. " Sam who was on our bedroom floor cutting out cardboard for the pop out bit, looks up at me and says, "Dusty, they're not like that here, they're different. We can win this. So stop sulking and help me." I'm bubbling up with anger as I spit out, "no, I'm not doing it, they're all the same and we can't win." Somehow this ensues into a scrap on the floor. My anger always ended with me scrapping with Sam, with us tearing chunks out of each other. The outcome was that Sam was going to continue to make the card on her own and I would make my own card that they deserved, without much effort put into it. Mine, was Santa in his sleigh flying through the sky with his reindeer. It was good enough, not a 3-D pop out Santa that Hallmark would have been proud to have in their shops. The winners were announced on the last day of school, before we broke-up for Christmas. And the prizes were given out personally to the children by Mr. Burke and Mr. Hastings, in Mr. Burke's office. The names of the children were announced over the intercom, by Mr. Burke himself. The excitement in his voice could not be contained he loved these competitions as much as the children. The winners were asked to come down to his office to receive their prizes. Sam had won first prize and was congratulated for such an imaginative and brilliant card by both Mr. Hastings and Mr. Burke. It was put in the glass display in the main hallway for everyone to see, with a big red first prize frilly bow next to it, so fitting for such a jolly Santa card. She was also given her own frilly red bow with 1st place written on the face of it, by Mr. Burke. And Mr. Hastings presented to her a rectangle box with a stainless steel pen seated inside, that also had a digital clock face embedded in the back end of the pen. I had never seen a clock in a pen before, it was beautiful, and I was gutted. Sam was right, they were different here. I had misjudged them. Just because they were teachers didn't mean they were going to be just like the ones in England.

Life seemed pretty good, I was learning so much. I was getting loads of certificates with scratch n sniff stickers on them, for doing so well, I loved it at school. And Sam was able to leave me at times and join the class with the advanced kids. She would come back for some lessons, so that I wouldn't miss her too much. Which looking back now, I realise how much this school cared for me, and did for me, as a vulnerable child. My speech was coming on too, since I had learnt the Alphabet and I was starting to be able to identify basic words and even write some. I was so happy. Lee had become my best friend, and we even got to see each other at weekends because our parents would take us over to each other's houses.

I hadn't had one wetting accident since I had arrived in Canada, life was great. Until one afternoon on the bus home, when I had forgotten to go to the bathroom before putting on my snowsuit and getting on the bus, and just as it starts to drive off I realise that I need a wee really bad. I had always had trouble with wetting myself. I was a day wetter, not the usual night-time bed wetter with an under developed bladder, to be honest there probably wasn't anything wrong with my bladder. It was just that I would get too engrossed in whatever I was doing at the time and would forget to go to the toilet. Sam notices me starting to do my wriggle wee dance in my seat, and she says to me "Dusty, do you need a wee-wee?" And I say, "No, I'm ok." Well, I could see it in her eyes, she knew and she thought it was funny, so she started to make me laugh by being extra silly in her comical ways. Since we moved to Canada our sense of humour did seem to get better and we could just about laugh at anything, and together we would have each other in stitches. Years later when we were teenagers our grandfather would say, we would laugh if our arses were on fire. Sometimes Sam would get the devil in her, our mother would say, and she did have it in her on this occasion. She knew I needed a wee and I told her to stop making me laugh, but she could not help herself. By the time the bus got to our stop I was in agony and I still had to try and get through three foot of snow first, in twenty below weather, to our apartment, and the bus stop was near the welfare apartments, which was a bit of a distance from ours. And when you need a wee that bad, it was already near on impossible, and with all the laughing Sam was making me do, I just couldn't make it. Sam was still laughing when she got off the bus, which was also making me laugh. I only got a few feet through the snow, and I just lost control of my bladder and wet myself. I could feel it down both my legs, in my trousers, and in my snowsuit, it was very warm at first, but then, it quickly began to freeze, and I tried to move fast through the snow drifts just to get home. It was making me very cold and sore. By the time I got to our apartment I was in tears because I was so cold, and the chafing had slowed me down too, it felt like it took forever to get back. I got to the upstairs door of our apartment and my mom opened the door to find me crying and she saw that I had wet myself. She was so sympathetic, she ran me a bath and put my clothes in the wash. The inside of my legs was frost bitten and sore. My mom asked me what had happened. I told her that, Sam was making me laugh, when she knew I needed a wee. She asked me where my sister was and I said, I thought she was here at home. My mom replied "no, she hasn't come back yet, the little devil, but she will wish she hadn't, when I get a hold of her." Just as my mother says that Sam comes through the door, she's still laughing. My mother clipped her around the head with her right hand, and sent her straight to her room. She was still laughing then, even after a smack. It turned out that she had lost balance from all the laughing, and had fallen in a snow drift; because she was in what had become uncontrollable fits of laughter, and wearing a children's snowsuit, she had gotten kind of stuck and had struggled to get up and out of the drift. For once she felt like the baby penguin struggling to get up and run away. That made it worse, she was crying with laughter, and that is where she had been the whole time. You see, for years my sister had been calling me the baby penguin. Whenever I would try to run she and many other people had said, I ran like a baby penguin. That was actually the last time I peed myself. I never once did it again because I never left home or school without going to the toilet first.

Why did my sister call me Dusty? My brother named me Dusty; he named me Dusty soon after I was born. My father, my mother's first husband had taken Alex who was six at the time to the hospital to meet his new twin sisters. When the nurse introduced us to him, he called Samantha, Sammy and when he was shown me, he said I was a Dusty, and should be put in the bin, the dusty bin. I didn't know my name was Justine until I was six years old. My entire family had up until that point, only ever called me Dusty, Dusty-bin, Dust-Dust or even Dust-bag but never once Justine. I was on holiday with my grandparents at Blackpool, back when we lived in England. It was the summer of 1978. They had taken us to see a matinee Pantomime, down at the North Pier. Before the show would start a stagehand would warm-up the audience and entertain the children, probably to keep them from tearing the place apart and to get them focused on the show, and how to interact with the Pantomime, like when to shout out, "He's behind you". The stagehand asked for children from the audience to come up. Sam, my cousin Antony, Alex and I all lifted our arms up so high we could have pulled them right out of their sockets. We were so excited and desperately wanted to be picked. We were the lucky children that had been picked and ran up on stage with great excitement. There we were stood on this grand stage; all lined up like the von Trapp children. The stagehand, a slim young man in his early twenties, asked for our names and ages starting with my brother who was to the right of me.

"And what is your name?"

"Alex". My brother says with a deep moody voice, right in the microphone the man is pointing at my brother's face.

"And how old are you?" Is, of course, the next question in this performance.

"Twelve" Say's my brother still with that moody Sheffield tone, of a soon to be teenager.

The man then moves on to my cousin.

"And what is your name?"

"Antony." My cousin mimics the moodiness of my brother in tone.

"And how old are you Antony?"

"I'm five" With the microphone shoved right under his mouth.

"And what is your name young lady?"

"Dusty". I say with great excitement in my little voice, for being up here in front of the entire world and his dog.

"That's a strange name for a little girl." The man says with humour in his northern voice.

My cousin shouts out to him. "That's not her real name, her real name is Justine but she doesn't know her real name".

Then Sam joins in, who is stood to the left of me and not had her turn yet. "That's because no one uses her real name we all call her Dusty or Dusty-bin or Dust-bag."

Everybody in the audience is laughing at me, like what has been said, is the funniest joke ever told. The laughter fills the theatre like a deep wave of over whelming condemnation of my ignorance. I felt deep shame and confusion. Why did I not know my name was Justine? Why had no one bothered to tell me? How come my cousin who was a year younger than me knew, and my sister, but not me?

The stagehand loves the reaction of the audience, and thinks he can milk this for all the laughs he can get. That was, until my sister realizes he's mocking me beyond compassion so she kicks him right in the shin and sticks out her tongue at the audience. I wanted the stage to swallow me whole, and save me from the world, that was laughing, without sympathy at my misfortune and ignorance. When I went to sit back down with my grandparents and family, my Nan was crying and had her hanky out to wipe away her tears, because I didn't even know my own name, and it was so pathetic and shameful.

My granddad said to her, under his breath because he didn't want anyone to notice his wife crying, or his attempt to rein her back in for it. "Betty, pack it in, your making it worse."

Betty, ignoring my granddad's request for her to stop the tears, said "That poor child doesn't even know her own name. What will become of her?"

Now I knew that my name was Justine, but this just caused me more problems in my life in England. I had a French man's name. People in England would then ask me, why did your parents give you a French name, a man's name at that, Justin that's not a good name for a girl? It wasn't until I moved to Quebec that I learnt to embrace my name, and learnt to love it, thanks to the French culture. I may not have fit in Quebec, but my name did, and I liked the way people would say it, with a French accent the way it should be said. The sound of my name, said by the French, felt like home.

Saint Jude School had brought in an educational psychologist for some of the children to be assessed. Sam and I were both chosen to see this lady and we went to see her individually and also she would see us together. These assessments, from what I can remember, were done in a very non-intrusive manner and were probably revolutionary at the time. We did the basics at first like color blind testing, and what we could count up too in English and French. We were asked to write a little story and I remember her saying to me, "it's ok if you can't spell words, just spell things the way you think they should be spelt." I was given math to do, I was shown a picture and had to talk about it. There were puzzles and problem solving involved as well. It went on for some time. She would have Sam join us at times, then proceed to ask me questions and just watch how Sam would answers for me, and protect me by stepping forward blocking the psychologists from my sight and talking for me. She watched how Sam and I would solve a problem together, like putting shapes into patterns, and watch how in situations like that, I would become more forward and help solve them. The psychologist would spend about forty-five minutes with us, each time. She would start the session by asking how we were feeling today. How we were getting on? and would chat to us in a very kind and understanding manner, not in a patronizing way like some adults tend to do.

I actually liked this woman; she made me feel special like my new teachers did. By the time she had finished doing her assessments and left; I missed her. Anyway, a letter came home to our parents during the school holidays, saying that this educational psychologist had been into the school and conducted this in-depth assessment on both Sam and I. And that the results were, that I was severely dyslexic, and speech delayed, and that I needed a lot of support with my education and that due to my form of dyslexia, learning French for me was going to be difficult, and may take years to grasp the basics, and that I would need a lot of help and understanding. It further stated that, Sam spent a lot of her time protecting me from others, and that is why she would speak and do things for me. It also stated that Sam had a mild form of dyslexia but that her level of intelligence was so high, that she had compensated for it, and that Sam needed a lot of stimulation to keep her interested, because she was a very intelligent child both academically and emotionally. The letter also explained that, Sam would have to be put in the higher group next year, to make sure that she was getting what she needed academically. This would help me, because it would allow me to learn without having Sam do things for me. They were aware of my emotional needs and would not completely separate us. We would have access to each other, whenever I needed it. I remember my parents and Alex reading this letter and talking to each other about it. They sat me down on the sofa and talked to me about it too. In a way it was a relief, because someone was able to tell me what was wrong with me, but there was no cure for it. They just said that I needed a lot of support from everyone and that the school was doing everything possible to help me.

Talking to my mom years later she told me that it was Mrs. Meehan that picked up my dyslexia straight away because she had been trained to. She had studied learning disabilities and dyslexia and it was she who requested that I be seen by the educational psychologist that came to the school. The way Mrs. Meehan taught me to read and write was by using many different techniques some helped and some not so much but it took time and a lot of work from both the teachers and I. It was exciting for me because a world was being unlocked and I was allowed to join it. For the first time, I could pick up a basic children's book and try and read it and I was helped by my teachers not punished when I couldn't.

The two years that Sam and I were in Saint Jude School we both flourished tremendously I could spell my name properly and a lot of one-syllable words like basic nouns and verbs. I had the reading and writing ability of a seven year old. In two years I had come so far and I had more confidence about myself. I was starting to get there after all.

All children are born to shine

But we will teach them whom to hate

(V)

"Man must evolve for all human conflict a method which rejects revenge, aggression and retaliation. The foundation of such a method is love."

Martin Luther King Jr.

Our experience with the Québécois children was not all great, in fact there was times when Sam and I had to run literally for our lives. The first time we ever had to run was in the summer soon after we had just moved to the Belleview area. Sam and I were playing at the back of our apartment building near the Welfare apartments just doing our own thing playing by ourselves. Sam just happened to look over in the direction that a chorus of charging, yelling group of people were coming from and saw that they were running towards us brandishing weapons in their hands and Sam screams, "Run". I looked up and could not believe what I was seeing. It was a gang of kids about fourteen of them, our age and older, running towards us from the direction of the welfare apartments with crowbars and baseball bats and bicycle chains in their hands. And they were going to kill us. I screamed and began to run for my life. By this time my sister had gone, she was like the wind. She was of course the fastest runner in our previous school in England and the whole neighborhood. I, on the other hand was like a baby penguin trying to run away from a bird of prey. Tears were streaming down my face and of course I stupidly kept looking back. If this had been a teen horror movie you know I would have been a dead chick. They were calling after us "les maudit anglais, les tete carre" (the bloody English the square heads) and of course my favourite, "cochons anglais" (English pigs). Luckily for me, Sam had left the downstairs door open, as I just made it in time and slammed the door shut behind me as I heard the French kids hit the door and begin to bang and kick at it. I swear to God I peed myself a little bit, I was that scared. My sister was already on the balcony of our apartment calling them "Fucking French bastards". One thing that got to me though, there were two boys that stuck out amongst the French kids, they're the redheaded boys from Scotland that lived in the apartment building next door to ours. They were also trying to kill us.

The next day when I was coming out of our building I bumped into the older one of the two boys, he was eleven years old, two years my senior and I said to him,

"What do you think you're playing at, ganging up on me and our Sam? Your bloody British like us, how come your hanging out with them lot and trying to kill us?"

The boy Jim was his name replies, "I'm not bloody British I'm Scottish and we Scott's hate you English just as much, if not more than the French, for what you have done to us for centuries, so you can fuck off back to England for all I care, you bastards."

Well that cleared that up. I had no idea that we were hated up in Scotland too. I had never met anyone from Scotland before. Would you like me to explain what the English had done to the Scott's as well? Well let's just say that murdering whole villagers and destroying people's souls and creating laws that meant that an English man was dutifully required to rape the Scottish women on the Scottish man's wedding night to ensure that a Scott's man blood line was bread out and replaced by an Englishman's as a form of punishment to the Scottish for standing up against the English had not been forgotten. Did you ever watch the movie *Brave Heart*, with Mel Gibson? That's about the gist of it. No wonder we were so hated it's difficult to feel much pride or any at all when you discover that the English have gone around the world conquering others and treating human beings with such contempt and hatred. Thanks to my life in England and the way I had been treated there, I was a child with very low self-esteem but now it had plummeted to an all time low.

My sister and I were in and out of scraps with that Scottish boy and his younger brother Andrew a few times, and to be fair he did scare us a lot because he was quite brutal and pretty hard. His hate for us just ran so deep we did what we could to stay out of his way but he was a shit. If we were outside playing and he came out we knew that if he could gather up the French kids in time they would come round wanting a fight with us so we used to have to keep our wits about us and move fast and get back inside the apartment behind the big doors where we were safe. Thank God he lived in the apartment building next door and not the same building or he would have just let the French kids in and we would have been killed. Alex didn't like him either he used to call him the "ginger tosser". He used to say he was as ugly as he was ginger and I took some comfort in the fact that my brother was older and bigger than this boy and that Alex would threaten him whenever he saw him.

One day almost two years later Sam and I were not so lucky I think my mom and Dad had gone out shopping and there was no one around to buzz us back into the apartment. It was the spring time of 1983 just before our eleventh birthday. The French kids had come for us again and we were cornered behind our apartment building on the big grass area that was like no man's land between the welfare apartments and the new private apartments that we lived in. There was no point in us running anymore, they had bikes and we had nowhere to run to. Back in England our mother's friend Tony had taught us self-defence which was based on Aikido and he always used to say to Sam and me, if you get a gang on you take out the biggest and the hardest, the gang leader and the rest will not touch you. We were both shaking. Sam told me to back her up, which I did, I stood my ground. One thing I did notice though is that they are not tooled up, thank God. They were not prepared and the Scottish boys are not with them. (When I look back as an adult I have thought about it and maybe they were so used to chasing us without success maybe they weren't expecting to catch-up with us that day or any other day for that matter, after all we were just kids, but then some days they did seem quite savage as they ran for us and would try and kick our door in). Sam was praying and asking God to help her because if she got this wrong they were all going to jump in and kill us both.

Sam shouts out with great confidence like she is the one in charge of this lynch party. "Who here is the hardest and is in charge of this gang?"

A boy steps forward. "I am," with his broken English, but sounding as confident as his Enemy.

Sam says, "Really"

As this boy starts to say something else, she punches him straight in the nose and then kicks him as hard as she could straight between the legs. He goes down like a sack of, well you know. She busted his nose and he's on the ground crying in pain Sam drops down on her knees and starts to ask this boy for forgiveness and is saying she's sorry.

Sam is rambling, "I'm so sorry that I hurt you. I know you hate me because I'm from England but I'm just a girl, I'm not a country."

"I'm not a politician, can't you leave politics to the grown-ups and can't we be friends?"

"We are just children, we don't have to be enemies, we could be friends if we want to be. I'm sorry I hurt you. I would like us to be friends."

I just stood there with his gang of lost boys thinking; well, he and the rest of them deserved this. We've spent almost two years running away from them and the bloody Scott's next door, even Michael and his sister have been occasionally caught up in all of this and until they had met us they had never had any trouble from the French kids before, because they themselves are half French. So it had become hard on them too. Sam picks him up off the ground and tells him to pinch his nose and she goes back to the apartment and buzzes our neighbor Cynthia who lives downstairs from us and asks her for some tissue. Sam goes into Cynthia's and comes back with a wad of toilet roll. The other French kids just seem to watch what is going on and do nothing and say little, nothing in English anyway. The boy and Sam begin to talk and exchange names and he introduces his brother to us, their names were Stephen and Benoit; they then introduced us to all of their gang. By the end of this day that we spent talking to these boys and their friends in their broken English I get the feeling that we won't be having any more trouble from them again. I was right we don't, but the Scottish boys still hate us and give us some grief but the French aren't going to bother us again in this neighborhood. In fact Stephen and Benoit start coming round on their Choppers to take us out for ice-creams and they would take us down to the local depanneur (depanneur comes from the French verb depanner meaning to help out of difficulty or you can just see it as French for local shops) which their family owned; for free ice-creams and candy. They would turn up at our apartment where my mother would be sunbathing on the balcony and say "Hello Mrs. Réussite can we take your daughters out for ice-cream"? My mother adored them she thought they were so well mannered. It turned out that their family, were members of the local separatist party and they were not happy that their boys were hanging round with English girls from England. But the boys didn't care what anyone said apparently we were their girlfriends and they treated us like we were princesses. Stephen was my boyfriend and he was quite cute and a lot older than me. I was eleven by this time and he was thirteen going on fourteen but he looked about my age he was quite small for his age. I think my mom would have gone mad if she knew how old they were. Stephen had beautiful dark olive skin and black hair brown eyes and gorgeous white teeth and I loved his smile and holding on to his body on the back of his bike. I even liked the smell of him. His brother Ben was dating Sam he was only twelve and his English was not as good as Stephen's but their English on the whole was really starting to come on since we started to hang out with them. They were the most lovely boys we had ever dated no one dared touch us now and I loved having a boyfriend and all the attention that went with it. We didn't have to walk anywhere now because they took us everywhere with them on their Choppers.

It was Friday 24 June of 1983 Saint Jean-Baptiste Day this is the National holiday of Quebec it is a day of celebration of the French culture. However over the years it had become an out let for the politically charged French Québécois to express their hatred and discontent towards the English speaking Quebecers and the Anglo-Saxon imperialist that they believed are responsible for all that is wrong with Quebec. It is a time when the English make themselves scarce in Quebec and avoid creating attention that the French could perceive as a slur on their culture and language or even an invitation to fight. The fleur-de-lis flags fly high and proud and the Canadian flags are nowhere to be seen. Emotions run high and the atmosphere is palpable. Stephen, Benoit, Nadine and Michael turned up at our apartment they wanted us to come out and celebrated with them. All of their families and friends were out there and they wanted us to join in and I remember saying, "I don't think it's a good idea because we're English and from England." Stephen said it would be ok as long as we didn't speak. That they would look out for us and protect us, that we would be safe. Sam and I wanted to share this day with them because we knew it meant so much. While my boyfriend and friends were having a wonderful time amongst the celebrations with the loud music and people that were drinking beer and eating carnival foods. The overwhelming smells of corn on the cob that was being handed out for free, mixed with the aroma of hotdogs, Cotton candy and Canadian beer induced an intoxicating sensation amongst the celebrators. We were surrounded by a chorus of laughter and chatting in French. As we move through the crowds I felt fear starting to take possession of me. I felt like an intruder and the effigy of all that they hated, that would, if not careful end up on the bonfire by the end of the evening. Being here had put me in jeopardy and I felt defenseless. The only part of me that belonged here was my name. I clung to Stephen's arm like it was a life raft; just hoping no one would try and speak to me. When friends and family of Stephen's did try to chat with me

Stephen told them I was a very shy girl and he would speak for me, Ben did the same for Samantha. I was already aware that his family didn't agree with our relationship, I felt judged and condemned. Neither Sam nor I felt safe, because we were all that they hated. We did stick it out for the entirety of the evening for the sake of our boyfriends and friends and when it came time for the bonfire and fireworks, effigies were placed on the mountain sized bonfire with a burning heat that even as I stood at a distance was uncomfortable on my face. I didn't ask what the effigies represented I could already guess for myself.

Years later in 2006 I remember hearing Shawn Mullins's song Shimmer for the first time while living in my apartment in Kent. His voice and the way he plays the guitar and even the way he looks just reminds me of my old teacher Mr. Hastings who would bring his guitar into class in Saint Jude's and sing to us children as a treat for doing well. He was so soulful and very cool with his long strawberry-blond hair, blue eyes and beard I don't know why but he carried that look off well, you know the disheveled look; he was such a cool guy. I was transported back by this song to Greenfield Park to the school Saint Jude, our teachers, to those children Michael and Nadine, all of our friends and the boys Stephen and Ben who had started their journey with us hating us and then by the end loving us. I think about the impact we all had on each other's lives and how as adults we are responsible for how our children will perceive this world, and the people in it that they will have to share this world with. I think about how Michael's and Nadine's parents had obviously taught their children to love and to shine and the children that wanted to kill us had been taught how to hate. Yet with their own experiences with Sam and I chose to love instead. All children are born to love and born to shine and as their guardians of them I feel it is a crime against humanity and God to teach them how to hate. I had received a phone call from my mother just weeks before to tell me that she had recently found out that one of our old school teachers from Saint Jude had passed away, Mr. Hastings, he had cancer. I was shocked to hear that a teacher that I cared for had died. Some years back I had gone to visit the school Saint Jude while I was over in Canada for a visit and had met up with Mr. Hastings who was then engaged to marry and to my surprise he had shaved off his beard which was great to see his face for the first time. His fiancée had convinced him that he could, that he no longer needed the beard to hide his scares and she was right you could hardly see the scares and he looked better for it. It just goes to show that sometimes time can heal our wounds and with love on our side we can let down our barriers and give ourselves a chance at something new. Mr. Hastings and Mrs. Meehan were the most loving teachers I had ever met. Mrs. Meehan loved every one of her children like a mother. Sometimes in class we would accidently call her mom and of course whenever a kid slipped up and did this, boy would they get ripped up by the rest of us. But you know I can't count how many times I made a Freudian-slip and called her mom and I didn't really care when I got my fair share of ribbing for it because she was like a second mom to me and to us all. Mr. Burke never told the other teachers about our true status in that school he kept that burden to himself it was not until many years later Sam and I were able to tell Mrs. Meehan the truth. Unfortunately he had past away from colon cancer by then. As I listen to the song "Shimmer" tears swell up and I begin to cry; now heaven has two more angels.

1981-1980 Cultural differences

(VI)

The past is our definition. We may strive, with good reason, to escape it, or to escape what is bad in it, but we will escape it only by adding something better to it."

Wendell Berry

The first few weeks at the new school in Quebec, Justine and I found a safe haven that was to repair a lot of damage done by our old school in England. We were sitting in our new classroom where everything here was colourful and bright, it felt modern and warm. We felt safe immediately, a feeling we had not had before and at the time I didn't know why we felt so good about this place but as we started to settle in, we soon figured it out. It was such a contrast to what we experienced in England, where the school Meersbrook Bank was Victorian in its appearance and Dickensian in its ethos and treatment of children. It was an antiquated Victorian building with cold stone walls. The tall Victorian style windows peer down on you like bullies in a playground. The large archaic piping and radiators in the class rooms and hallways that once, a long time ago, had been painted white, in an attempt to help them fit into the building and blend into the dreary decorum, made the building feel colder in character, despite the heat that ran through them during the winter months. It felt grey, dark, cold, hopeless and frightening. I remember pain and fear when I look back on that place.

My sister Justine had learning difficulties. In those days they called her retarded and I heard them saying that she shouldn't be in the school with the other children, it left me feeling afraid that they would take her away from me. You see I couldn't comprehend why people couldn't understand Justine like I did. I wondered at times if it was that they didn't try hard enough. I knew her every thought just by looking at her face and understood every word that came out of her mouth. My mother would say it's because we are twins and that we had our own twin language and that was the only language Justine was capable of speaking. I would notice that people couldn't understand her and then they would be quick to dismiss her so I would interject quite quickly and speak for her so that she would be heard and understood. The teachers were scary cruel people to me that would hit us often and say nasty things about our mother and our social class. They wanted us to know every day we were not liked by them and that we did not belong. You see our mother was divorced to our biological father whom we never saw. My mother then remarried a man four years younger than her. She had originally married a man twenty years older than herself at a very young age and of a different social class. She was working class and he was a man of the upper class that had come from a good family and he had attended the right sort of boarding schools. Which meant he spent most of his life in a school far away from the love and warmth of his parents, he came home only at Christmas, Easter and summer holidays, apparently that's the way to raise a true great English man, you know the sort that run the world. My personal opinion on that one is, you wonder why the English are so emotionally disconnected and brutal to the rest of the world at times, love must start at home with the parents. They were really worlds apart a girl raised by parents on a daily basis in her own village surrounded by a community who watched her grow into a young woman and the two should never have married. My teachers knew this and would gossip about my mother with each other but of course children would over hear them including Justine and I.

We knew we were not liked because we were half breeds and our mother was a divorcee which was very frowned upon.

Our teacher Mrs. Nailer was a tall skeletal old woman with chiselled features of despair and hunger, whose whole being had been eaten alive by all the hatred and bitterness in the world. In plainer words she was the grim reaper but without the cloak and scythe. Mrs. Nailer would insist that my sister should sit under the black board because she was retarded instead of sitting at her desk like a normal child and whilst Mrs. Nailer would write on the black board she would kick my sister in the back causing her awful pain and bruising in her kidneys. To watch Justine being treated like that was humiliating it was like she was the class room dog, not a child but a mangy mutt forced to know its place, its position in the class room and in society. How could anyone do this to a child? It was inhumane. I would look at her frail body hunched over, head bowed so low it was no longer visible from behind. She was forced to face the front wall; her back was to always face the class. And if she was not far enough under the easel Nailer would kick at her and push her further under with her ugly black court shoes like she was nothing more than an animal that needed to obey. It took sometime before Justine even told me she was being kicked. The persecution had escalated since Nailer had refused to teach Justine any longer. When it was reading time and the children would go one at a time to read to the teacher, Justine was excluded from this. I shall never forget the day that Nailer took away my sisters rights to be human, when she destroyed a child and made her the class pet.

My sister went up to her one day and said to Mrs. Nailer. "Miss, you fer-forgot me, it was my t-turn." She stuttered as best she could.

Mrs. Nailer retorted. "No I haven't forgotten you. You're not worth teaching, you shouldn't even be here. You are a waste of my time. Now go and sit down because I will not waste any more of my time on trying to teach you. In fact from now on you can sit under the blackboard so I don't have to put up with you."

I not only heard this I saw my sister's face and I saw a little soul starting to die. It killed me inside and at that moment I vowed I would find a way to make it stop and protect my sister. It was late at night when Justine would climb in my bed because she was scared of the dark in fact she was scared of pretty much everything; it was then that she would tell me her fears and then she would tell me how she didn't like being kicked in the back by the teacher as she sat under the easel. She would cling to me with all her pain and fear and tell me she wanted it to stop. I would promise her that somehow I would find a way to make it stop and that I would protect her forever.

In her little voice she would ask "Will you Sammy, protect me forever and never leave me or let them take me away?"

"Forever Dusty, I will protect you and they won't take you away from me, I promise, it will be ok, I will make it better."

It was then that something in me changed I became hardened and full of hate for anyone who looked down their noses at Justine and I, and I became dangerous.

I had recently developed a close friendship with two brothers that were a little older than us; they were the Wright boys, Marc and Richard. Bad boys that were always trouble. These lads hated our teacher as much as we hated her. We decided to just get rid of her. We went into the school garage where her car was parked. We then loosened and removed all the nuts on her wheels. We prayed it would kill her but God doesn't answer those sorts of prayers. The next day an assembly was called by the headmaster Mr. Elliott and Mrs. Nailer. To our great disappointment she was alive and angry. That evening when she drove out of the grounds all the wheels had come off her car down Meersbrook Park road. Like a scene out of a *Carry On* movie, wheels disappearing in all directions north, south, east and west and her in the driver's seat with a face like a slapped arse going nowhere fast but to the nearest garage. But no serious injuries to her or anyone else, lucky old cow. I was eight years old at this point and so full of hate for people like her. I really felt that there was no coming back from this. They asked the students in the assembly to come forward with information about who had tried to kill her and vowed that we would be punished. The Wright boys and I looked at each other with disgust. We couldn't believe she was alive and well. There was no chance in hell anyone in this school would be giving them that information. The few that knew hated that woman and were also disappointed in her survival. There were children they would check and those they wouldn't. We knew this so others helped with the disposal of evidence, which meant the nuts were pocketed and chucked in neighbour's bins on the way home from school. Only a couple of weeks earlier Mrs. Nailer and I had come to blows, and of course with how she was treating Justine, I was high up on the list of suspects. Mrs. Nailer was staring right at me and my gang. She knew who had done it. You could see it in her nasty old face. All twisted up, her lips pursed and her beady eyes attempting to penetrate our souls to drag the truth out of us. Like a Salem towns man drawing the witch from the child's body. Like that would make us crack. The truth would not be discovered no matter how impressive a witch hunt they put on. The circumstantial evidence was pointing right at me and my gang. We had the means and the motive. She knew alright but they had no evidence and no witnesses. You see to even make it into our gang you had to be made of strong stuff; cowards were quickly weaned out in the initiation process.

One of our run-ins was when I was sitting in class minding my own business doing my work and a girl next to me, Debbie, asked me a question. I had quietly retorted, "be quiet I'm trying to do my work." Mrs. Nailer then jumped in, not only to chastise me verbally but to punish me physically. This happened too often and I grew to hate this woman and her persecution of us. She would accuse me of doing wrong when I hadn't. Then I would have to have the slipper bare bottomed bent over in front of my class mates. The girl Debbie wouldn't get the slipper because her mother sold Avon to Mrs. Nailer. They were friends and worked on the PTA together so I had to be punished instead. I got up and went to the front of the class pulled my trousers and pants down and bent over to touch my toes this was the required position for the slipper or cane. Mrs. Nailer liked the slipper and the ribbed type; it would pull at your bare skin when she hit you with it. It was more painful than the plain flat slipper. Looking back now as a mother and a grown adult I realise that this woman should have been locked up for what she had done to us. I remember the humiliation of being naked and bent over feeling vulnerable about my nakedness and exposed to everyone in the room. I wanted it to pass as quickly as possible, the urge to pull my pants and trousers up as fast as I could to recover from that violation. To this day I refuse to touch my toes I don't like how it feels to bend over in that position. She gave me the slipper ten times. I was in a lot of pain but would not shed a tear and would not cry out, it was dishonourable to cry. I could never forget fellow class mate Paul crying whilst getting the slipper, it was so shameful. I would not cry. Every time I got the slipper I showed my class mates that I was strong. After I pulled up my pants and trousers and was walking back to my desk I said "That didn't hurt Bitch." I thought I had said this in my head but the look of fear and horror on every child's face told me to my great disbelief that I had said this out loud, very loud. Their faces were painful to look at some looked as if they were starting to cry for me. The teacher screamed out loud, "What did you say?" I knew it was out there and I couldn't take it back. The only option was to own it proudly and turn around to her and say it again loader and clearer, so that's what I did. "That didn't hurt bitch and you heard me the first time." She said she was going to teach me a lesson and how dare I say such a disgusting thing and she was going to beat it out of me. And so she tried, she gave me the slipper again, over and over again. I can't tell you how many times but I know I wanted to scream but I wouldn't let myself. I wanted to cry but I would not let that woman break me. I went back to my desk. I could not sit but pretended to, leaning my weight onto my forearms on my desk trying to keep my blistered bottom of the chair. Every child in the class room looked at me with so much sympathy I could tell they felt for me but there was nothing they could have done to save me. At break time I was sent down to see the Head Master to tell him what I had done and have my name put in the little black book that they said follows you on to secondary school. I went down to his office, went into see him and even pulled my trousers and pants down to offer him to beat me some more, because I assumed that he would want to also punish me for saying what I had said to Mrs. Nailer. He looked at my blistered bottom and said that he felt I didn't need any more of the slipper. I was relieved. He just wrote something in his black book about what I had done to the teacher, calling her a bitch. I was angry inside I didn't feel like I deserved to be in that book. So you can imagine after that incident I was at the top of their list of suspects. But I knew they had nothing on me, evidence wise and no child had come forward. My gang of criminals and I had gotten away with attempted murder.

Some days later after "The Bitch" incident and the "attempted murder" incident I had another run in with Mrs. Nailer. A girl in my class called Donna who had persistently teased me about my mother had complained to her mother that I had slapped her in the face. This was true, I had. She was picking on me, continuously saying awful things about my mother. They may have been true what she said but it still hurt. This girl originally wanted to be friends with me about a year ago; however her parents said she was not allowed to have anything to do with us because our mother was a divorcee and the wrong sort. We weren't allowed to go to her birthday parties or play with her after school. This was the same for a fair few children whose parents felt like that about my mother being divorced. Justine and I were aware that this was just the way it was because of our mother and grew to accept it. But what I wasn't putting up with after a prolonged period of time was being teased about this and being made to feel less of a person because of this. The truth is you do start to feel less of a person once you are pushed out of society and told you're not good enough. When push comes to shove, when you are bullied as well as pushed out you start to fight back because you feel like you have nothing left to lose. So you may as well fight back to stop the bullying.

I had Donna up against a wall near my house by the throat and then after I asked her to stop this persistent torment. I slapped her across the face, hoping that this would put an end to it. I hated doing it but I thought it would make it stop. The next day her mother came down to the school and was speaking to Mrs. Nailer just outside the classroom. I could see them talking but had no idea what it was about, then Mrs. Nailer came back into the classroom and asked for Justine and I to join her outside. We did as we were told, still puzzled as to why. Mrs. Nailer told us that Donna's mother had come to the school to report that we had hit her daughter. She asked if this was true. I said yes that I had but that it was not at school so it was not school business. I tried arguing my defence that Donna had been tormenting me and that it had been going on for some time that this should be taken up with my mother not my teacher. They both looked at each other and Donna's mother made a derogatory remark about my mother, "that woman, there is no dealing with her." The teacher agreed. I also said that Justine had nothing to do with it but they didn't seem to care for a defence for her. Mrs. Nailer told me that she was going to give me and Justine the slipper in front of the whole school to teach us a lesson, not to be such awful bullies. I couldn't believe it, I was being punished for standing up for myself from the torment and bullying I had been facing from this girl and the only reason why she disliked me so much was because her mother had taught her to. As I pulled my sister behind me to protect her I said to Mrs. Nailer, "You will not hit me or my sister, ever again and every time you try to hit me or Justine I will hit you back for each hit I get or Justine gets you will get one and even for trying to hit either one of us. Then I am going to see the Head Master Mr. Elliot and I'm going to tell him what I've done and why and then I'm going to take my sister out of this school with me and then I'm going to send my mother down to deal with you, and nobody wants to deal with my mother. You will wish you had never been born when I send my mother down here." Mrs. Nailer was furious that I could threaten her. Her face became contorted with her disgust in me, she spat out her response to my threat.

"How dare you speak to me like that? You little madam."

She grabbed me by the arm to pull me into her to smack my bottom in anger. In defiance I spun round and punched her.

"I meant what I said. Every time you try to hit me or my sister you will get hit, then we're leaving so it's up to you. You leave us alone or this is how it will be. I am either going to take my sister and go to the Head Master's office now and then go home and send my mother down or I am going back into class with my sister and you are to never touch us again, this is your last warning".

Looking back on this I realise I should have told my mother everything but I didn't and that's children for you. Children don't think like adults even the most intelligent ones. We think like children and that is why a lot of abuse was able to happen back then without parents truly being aware of what was happening to their kids.

I looked at her hard straight in the eyes, I was not backing down and I meant every word. Her face revealed the dissemination, the dissolution of her power, she was defeated. She had no more control over me. I had gone rogue due to her abuse and there was no way she could rein me back in. I felt powerful and free. I decided to take my sister back into the class. I knew that I had things under control with this woman, her reign of abuse and bullying was over. If she dared to hurt my sister again she knew what the consequences would be.

My parents had been talking about moving to Canada around this time. It wasn't definite yet but it was a possibility. I remember being hopeful about moving any where really. I was sick of my life here in Sheffield. I hated school it was a dread, the place looked and felt like a prison. The teachers were rotten, cruel and cold hearted women that looked down their noses at me and my sister. At times I used to say to God if I don't get out of here soon I will never finish my education. I will become so rogue, I will leave school very young. I could not foresee myself doing well academically if I remained in that school or in that area of England. I had had enough. I had always believed at a very young age that I was going to do a lot academically. I would tell anyone who would listen that I was going to go to university and that I would study people, politics and law. It was my life plan and it had always been with me. I was born with this plan but the ignorance of this school and the people in the area I found to be a problem and I feared that they could potentially interfere with this, especially if I was to quit school at a very young age because of them. My anger at being mistreated by the teachers and the feeling of not being accepted by children because of their parent's disapproval of my mother had got the better of me. The children started to respect my rebellious behaviour and saw me as the girl who was not to be messed with, which made me feel even more empowered, but this snow balled and I was looking for a fight with teachers or anyone who I perceived to be a threat. It was just before my ninth birthday I was not certain yet if we were moving to Canada. The anger inside me towards this school and my life in Sheffield was growing stronger by the day. I felt this need to just get it out. It was a spring day in early April and quite sunny but not hot, I climbed up on the school wall because we were not allowed to. I was looking for trouble with the teachers so I climbed up and sat on the wall and I began to sing the song that I liked at the time it meant so much to me because of how I felt about this school and how the teachers had treated me, my sister and other fellow students. The song was by Pink Floyd *"Another brick in the Wall"* Other children climbed up onto the wall as well and began to join in. The dinner ladies told us all to get down and then came Mrs. Nailer she shouted at us all to get down and the children did but I refused and I kept on singing, "We don't need no education.... We don't need no thoughts control ....no dark sarcasms in the classroom ....teacher leave them kids alone ....Hey Teacher leave them kids alone....all in all you're just another brick in the wall." As I was singing this the Head master came out and also told me to get down but I wouldn't. I sang it at them as load as I could and I didn't get down until I had finished. I thought what can they do to me? Nothing was my answer because I won't let them touch me anymore and if they try then I will leave and I won't come back. So I no longer feared them and I would do as I pleased. I was full of anger towards them and I was letting them know it by humiliating them in front of other students showing them that they could not control me nor could they touch me. They knew this, so when I finished singing I just got down off the wall smiled at them and said "I'm finished now" and walked off back to the playground in the opposite direction of them just simply dismissing them. The Head Master turned to walk back into the school as did Mrs. Nailer they knew there was no point in trying to punish me they didn't want the battle. I was considered incorrigible. It was soon after this episode at school I found out that we were moving to Canada and I remember feeling relieved that I was leaving this school and this area of Sheffield behind. I had hope for a better life where I would not have to fight against the persecution I felt here.

An Education in History

The Bishops House Museum

(1980-1981)

(VII)

"Never think that war, no matter how necessary, nor how
justified, is not a crime."

Ernest Hemingway

We were eight years old and we had nothing to do all summer
because the military along with the police and fire service had
taken our monster away from us. We had a gang in the rough
part of Meersbrook Bank, Sheffield. To be in our gang you
had to urinate behind a certain tree and go into the stream and
touch a spike on the monster which of course proved bravery.
Being that some kids didn't want to do the blood brother
initiation because they were afraid of the cutting of fingers
with a knife this new form of initiation was decided. My
brother had passed this on to us, it was a hand me down gang

and we were the new generation. Justine and I would have preferred the shed and share of blood but other kids preferred the "urinate" behind the tree and touch the monster initiation. The reign of fear our great monster had over the brook where us children spent most of our time, came to an end the day a child that was too scared to touch the monster to join our gang ran home crying and told his mother. He had sworn that he had touched it; however my sister was adjudicating and insisted he had not, thus reducing the boy to tears. Little did we know was that our great monster was far more dangerous than we could have ever imagined. The following day police, fire-fighters and military showed up to take our monster away. There it was just being hoisted away like it was nothing more than a mennis. It looked humiliated and captured, its once massive round body and devious spikes now looked impotent and limp in comparison to what it had been to us, when it was free laying in the stream in waiting for its victims. It was said that it was a bomb left over from the Second World War. We turned up to see the area all cornered off and the fire-fighters were hoisting it away right out of the stream. That was it, our monster was taken away. What were we to do now and what war had this come from anyway? And how did a bomb from a war many years ago just live unnoticed by adults for so long? All of us kids knew about it. What was all the fuss about now? It had been our monster for years every kid in the neighbourhood knew about it. A big disappointment to us all but it got me thinking about this war that people still talked about.

Because our gang area had been cornered off Justine and I decided to take a stroll further up the park until we came across a cottage which we had never noticed before. Maybe it was because we had not come this far into the park before or we had been distracted by play. I don't know but that day of all days was to teach me so much.

We wondered through the park and came across an old house that looked like a mysterious and magical cottage to us. It was like we had just stumbled upon the witch's gingerbread dwelling in the Hansel and Gretel fairy tale. Its slightly crooked frame half timber supported by brick was intriguing and alluring. The contrasting black and white stripes and decretive detail was enough to set any child's imagination on fire. What child could resist? It was in fact a museum that was of the Tudor era, The Bishops House Museum. Historically it was a place where scythes were made. It is only too bad they didn't sell them on the way out; we could have picked one up for Mrs. Nailer. We dared to enter in and paid the admission price. We were in awe, it was a wonder and like nothing we had seen before. It was the closest we had ever gotten to stepping back in time and experiencing another world. Habitable rooms locked in a specific point in time so that others could experience the wonder of what once was. In this wonder of a place we found all kinds of historical stories and objects of great interest, not just of the house itself but many different periods of history from Tudor until the Second World War. There was a room that was dedicated to the two Wars. It had photographs of the concentration camps and the beaches of Normandy in the awfulness of the destruction, with the faces of those that had survived. There were uniforms of the military and the medals that represented their ordeal and battles. It became our second home that summer, we were there every day so much so that they stopped charging Justine and I entrance fees.

We would pack a lunch in the morning. As soon as my feet touched my bedroom floor I would be thinking of the museum and all that it had to teach me. Justine and I would make our own jam sandwiches and we would also pack a flask of orange cordial that sometimes would leak and get soaked up by our sandwiches so we would be left with soggy jam and orange cordial sandwiches. We would wrap up some custard cream biscuits in tinfoil and put a couple of packets of crisps in as well and an apple each. Once we were packed up and dressed we would set off on foot to the museum. There were books for us to read that I found very educational and fed that need in me that I had to learn about the history of man. War reveals the darkest nature of man that usually hides in the shadows, and yet so quickly unveiled when justified through politics. Justine of course would sit and listen intensely as I would read to her, because it was how she would learn too, through me.

This cottage became our school where for the first time we could learn. The people that worked there were kind to us and they came to know us by our first names. We were there every day from the minute they opened; they could have set their watches by our arrival. You would have been forgiven for thinking that we lived there. We would share our knowledge of the cottage's history with the daily visitors. We even brought our gang up to the museum but they were not as in awe about its presence as we were. So it became just our little sanctuary, a home away from home. And a school like no other.

I remember one particular day the elderly lady that had become quite fond of Justine and I came to ask if we would like to sit in on a presentation that had been made on the Holocaust. Usually children were not allowed because the subject matter was more serious than our years would have allowed us to comprehend. But because she had spent so much time teaching us about history and in particular the Second World War she thought that we were so enthusiastic we would benefit from the experience. Before the presentation began she explained our presence to the audience of elderly ladies and gentlemen and told them that she had spent a great deal of time with us over the summer months and that we were avid historians despite our youth. We had never had anyone speak so well of us before that in itself was something. It made us feel like we belonged there with them. That was until the audio tapes that played alongside the slide show began to reveal a very personal and highly emotional experience of the tragedy that was the Holocaust. Then tears began to stream down many of the faces of the audience. It was then that I felt like an intruder on their personal grief. To hear the voices of the victims on those tapes of the Holocaust, their personal experiences, it revealed an evil about the human condition that just wasn't there in the history books. The tapes revealed the true pain, the true horror of war that you can only hear from the voices of the survivors. I felt very privileged to have been allowed to be in that room and share that experience with these adults. What came from that experience was that evil knew no bounds and didn't discriminate unlike bigotry itself. It was an epiphany. I realised that anyone could be subjected to persecution for any reason. Anyone that opposed that evil would find themselves subjected to it also.

Pointe-Claire and Reality

(VIII)

"There is no doubt that it is around the family and the home that
all the greatest virtues, the most dominating virtues of human
society, are created, strengthened and maintained."

Winston Churchill

Unfortunately for me my parents decided to move to Pointe-Claire after just two years in Greenfield Park in 1983. Pointe-Claire is on the north shore of Lac Saint Louis. My parents had decided to finally buy a house, my dad had a new job and wanted to be closer to work and felt that it was time to put down proper roots and my mom wanted to move somewhere that was more Anglophone, (English speaking people and English friendly). This was very important to her.

I remember her saying, "maybe I could settle better if there were more English people around so I wouldn't feel threatened all the time."

Looking back I get that. And when people have made very ignorant statements to me about other groups of people like Asians, Africans, African-Caribbean's and Eastern Europeans, arguing that they are not like us and that they don't want to live with us, they just want their own communities like they have back in their own countries. I have been able to tell my story of how my mother and all of us felt and how we needed to feel secure and therefore felt that we needed to live closer to other English people like us to feel safe and at home. It has given me great insight and for that I am truly grateful to Quebec.

I remember an English man in England saying to me as a retort to a debate on immigration behavior, "yeah well us English don't go off to other countries and all live in one house or flat where there is already ten people or more living in there and sleep on floors and rotate beds like animals, so were nothing like them." My response was, "really you think so? Friends of mine did when travelling with other young English people from all over the world such as America, Canada, Australia and England. Some rotated beds and found English communities and due to finances lived on floors in cramped apartments and worked God awful jobs to get by." Samantha in her mid twenties by now, soon after she got back from Japan, said to me, when you're in a foreign country you're the Asian. You live together in small communities and live in poor conditions just to get by." This is just human nature and according to Abraham Maslow who describes the hierarchy of needs we will all do this. Safety is just as important to all human beings. It is a basic need that must be gained before we can then move forward with attaining our life goals and aspirations.

So the decision was made, goodbye Greenfield Park and hello Pointe-Claire. This was a decision I was going to regret my parents making. They had found a house that they could rent from an Indian couple that were like us, landed immigrants that had settled here some years back and had a young family themselves. This couple had wanted to move to a bigger house and was willing to rent this one out to our parents with the option of buying later if they wanted. They were very hospitable people and seemed very kind they even allowed us to have pets and as we all know that's a big ask of landlords. I remember they had invited us all over for dinner to get to know us before renting out the house to my folks. The wife had made all of this gorgeous food that was authentic Indian, with spices I had never experienced before and she had made so much. It was a very enjoyable evening and they told us many stories of their home land India and we in exchange told them many about our home land England and how we had found life here in Canada to be for us. This was the first Indian couple I was to meet in my life, and that were of an arranged marriage, that had a happy ending to their story, because they had fallen deeply in love with each other and were truly grateful for that blessing, because they had friends and members of their family that had not been as lucky as them to have fallen in love with their partners. I remember my dad and this man had a lot in common because they were both engineers and so had a lot to talk about. My mom and his wife got on quite well and I remember it being an interesting night filled with a lot of chatting and laughing. They were obviously happy with us because they rented the house to my parents not too long after the visit.

There seemed to be a lot more English Canadians in Pointe-Claire which made our whole family feel more at home. Sam and I were soon to make friends in the neighborhood and so were our parents. There was a big shopping mall nearby our house called the Fairview Mall and there was even a cinema. The neighbors all took turns to come and welcome us to the neighborhood there was even a welcome wagon lady that turned up with a basket of food to give us an official welcome to the neighborhood, it was a very English Canadian way of being. My dad answered the door to this lady she had a strong German accent saying, "Hi I am Olga and I am her to velcome you from the velcome vargon."

My dad responds "pardon?"

So she repeats what she has just said verbatim. Sam and I are standing right next to our dad at the front door; we're not quite sure what she is saying either. Then François shouts, "Julie I think this is for you."

My mom turns up and says, "Yes Frank what is it?"

"I can't understand a word she is saying." This was one of my dad's poorer qualities when it came to social etiquette and the meeting and greeting of strangers.

Sam and I are a bit embarrassed by this point.

Then my mom says to her, "sorry, can I help you?"

"Hi, I am he-are to velcome you from the velcome vargon ve are a local community association that velcomes all knew families into the area."

She hands my mother a great big basket, it was beautifully wrapped in cellophane with a big yellow bow, and within it was a combination of food, wine and chocolates.

My mom says with reserved surprise in her voice. "Oh, thank you, this is very kind of you, please come in and I'll put the kettle on."

The blond haired blue eyed lady with the German accent comes in and takes a seat in the kitchen amongst all the boxes and bundles of newspaper because we are still unpacking. She tells us all about the neighborhood and what facilities there are available to us. We were saddened to hear there is no local pool like what we had at Greenfield Park but she enjoyed telling us all about the local Library and the Mall. She was quite friendly and welcoming and it was a nice break from unpacking. I loved it. I remember thinking things were looking up now that we were living with English Canadians.

There were so many English children to play with in this new neighborhood we were able to make new friends the same day we moved in. We spent the whole summer playing tennis on the road at the side of our house. Our house was situated on the corner of the street. The area we played tennis happened to be just outside the home of one of our new friend's Nicky. There were hardly any cars back then so we could play for hours before we had to call, "car" and move out of the way. Could you imagine your kids doing that today? My mom and dad took us down to the sports store in the mall and bought us a tennis racket each. We were over the moon.

After living in the new neighborhood for only two weeks Nicky asked me out. I was thrilled because I was only playing tennis as I had a mad crush on this boy. He thought we had a lot in common because we were both mad about tennis. Nicky was the same height as me and he had dark brown hair, beautiful blue eyes that sparkled like gemstones and olive skin, he was of Italian decent. His parents were from Italy and didn't speak English very well but did slightly better with their French. His older sisters were trilingual and were very protective of their baby brother and I remember his cousin lived right next door to him. Late in the evenings after spending hours playing tennis with pretty much the entire neighborhood of children that were big enough to hold a racket in their hands, Nicky and I would lie on his front lawn and look up at the stars. The aroma of the warm grass that lay beneath our bodies mixed with the humid heat that was the air surrounding us, transfused with the gentle harmony of the crickets made his lawn the most welcoming of retreats after a long day of tennis. Nicky would hold my hand in his across his chest and I could feel his heart beat through my hand. He introduced me to every constellation the sky revealed, spent every late evening reviving the mythology that lived and breathed in the days of the Babylonians, Greeks and Romans, stories that have been passed down through time from father to son, stories that are now as distant to us mortals as the stars themselves. Nicky showed me a world that fed my imagination and the need in me to know more about this mysterious world that I had only recently joined. A world that was much bigger than even the greatest men and minds that it had ever known and would know and I loved him for that. Nicky's hands would orchestrate the sky like he was commanding a symphony and every so often his hands would reach back down and gently take hold of the golden cross around his neck which he would lift up to his mouth and kiss as though he was kissing Jesus goodnight before he would then turn his head to kiss me on my forehead as his beloved one.

My mom adored Nicky and his family and his mom would make us some of her mouth watering homemade pastries and her husband would bring them round with some of his homemade wine and sausages and in return my mother would take over her homemade cakes and buns. Our families developed a loving friendship based on family and food. I do remember Nicky's father trying to warn my dad as he pulled our father to one side, an attempt to be more discrete, in his limited English, that some of the people around here were not that good and to be careful, which was funny because by the end of this summer we were to find out what he was trying to warn us about. Nicky would carry with him the delicious aromas of his mothers cooking on his clothes as he would walk out of his door to come and meet us for a game of tennis or for a walk down to the local park. His mother made the best pasta sauce the world had ever tasted and her pastries were even better.

At first I thought that Pointe-Claire was a good move that was until my parents went to speak to the principal of the local English school; this principal wanted no part in accepting Sam and me in his school illegally, it was not a chance he was willing to take. I couldn't believe it; my life felt like it was coming crashing down. How was I going to cope? I could hardly speak English or even read and write the basics. I remember my parents coming home from meeting with this principal and my mother was upset and crying about it all, that she couldn't get us in an English school again like she had managed the last time. My mother was saying that she wished that we had never moved here to Pointe-Claire and that she had thought it would be a better place for us all, and that she couldn't believe that these people weren't willing to help us. It had put my dad in a bad mood too and he was saying to her.

"You wanted to move here Julie. The kids were settled in Saint Jude's but it was you who wanted to move, not me, you, and so here you have it, you're here. Why should that man put his job on the line for us? It's his job, his life you're asking to sacrifice here. As Mr. Burke said, it was too much even for him. He said it himself, he wouldn't do it again because there is no guarantee that no one will find out; he could have gone to prison and lost everything, that is what you are failing to understand."

This is a very valid point, Mr. Burke had talked to this man before my parents had gone to see him and he did say to him that he felt sorry for us and had taken us in illegally but had he the chance to do it again, he would have not done so because there is no guarantee of anyone finding out, after all this other principal now knew and maybe even other members of his staff. He put this argument to the other principal and said that he should consider it because in just one more year we would be going to high school and who would be taking us in then? It would mean involving another school, another principal and faculty that's a whole lot of people having to keep a secret and to have to trust with your careers' and lives.

Julie retorts, "And what about my daughters how are they going to survive this?"

François responds. "Well there's little choice they have to go to a French school and that is it, admittedly Justine is going to struggle, yes, but Sam will fly through it, it won't affect her one bit."

My mother losing the argument, raises her voice, her temper is showing through now. "You bloody French are all the same, you would side with them wouldn't you? You French bastard, my father warned me, he said all you French are the bloody same when push comes to shove you stick together. You're no different to the rest of the bastards over here".

My dad snaps back. "You're talking shit Julie; you're just pissed off because you're not getting your own way this time because Mr. Burke got in there first and told him his side of things and that principal thought better of it."

Julie spits back. "You fucking French bastard".

"French, fuck you Julie, I was born in England and raised in England my name maybe French and my family are French, my father's French yeh! But you are not lumping me in with the rest of them."

"Life for you here is just great, you fit in, your name fits and you look bloody French you are not persecuted like what we are because they all love you, because you're from the old country, you're a real French man". My mom is shouting louder now.

Dad argues back in his defence. "Julie, that is balls and you know it, when people speak French to me I ask them to speak to me in English, just like you, I am no different to you."

"But you are different you look French, your name is French and you speak French. You can survive it here; you're not being persecuted for being English like the rest of your family."

Dad's voice lowers a little now. "Do you think for one minute I want my daughters to go through this? I don't, but we all have no choice it's the law like it or hate it, we have to get on with it, they are going to a French school".

I was so sorry that my parents were arguing over this. I didn't want that. But looking back on that fight, I find it funny that we all can become bigots when life isn't going our way, we can take it out on even the one person we love and are supposed to care about the most. My mom went upstairs and cried it out on her bed and my dad gave her a bit of time before he went up and comforted her.

A few days later one of the neighbors informs my mom that she could put me in a private English school legally. So my mom broaches the subject with my dad that night when he gets home from work. François wasn't interested, he said there was no way he was paying for me to go to a private school that he didn't have the money and he would not pay for a school that in his opinion was no better than a state school. My mom was arguing that he had missed the point that it would save me from going to French school but he didn't want to know.

François, "No private school would want a severely dyslexic child who is also speech delayed anyway, because they would affect their academic results." He then said, "They wouldn't have her; you wouldn't even get her through the front door."

My mom is trying to plead her case. "It would only have to be for a year then we could switch to a state school the following year".

Under Bill 101 students who attended private English schooling for a year became eligible to enter the public English school system. My dad just wouldn't have it. He wasn't going to even look into it, so they started arguing again and it was worse than the last argument. My dad may have been right about this because private schools do have entrance exams you need to take to even qualify for a place in their schools. As a severely dyslexic child I would not have had a hope in hell of passing an entrance exam for a private school; not even money could fix this. My dad was hoping to buy a house the following year and this was going to be a struggle to achieve because they had still not fully recovered from the financial hardship since his redundancy with the engineering company that brought us over to Canada. He was unfortunately made redundant after one year of employment; although he had a new job it would be a long time before they would be financially right again. What I can tell you today about the private school loophole is that in 2002 this exemption in the Bill 101 was closed up by the Bill 104 which has now been replaced by Bill 115. This is a complicated law that will ensure that your child will not be able to attend an English public school.

Late that summer when all of us kids were down the park one evening it was coming up to about ten at night but it was the summer so the sun had not gone in yet so neither did we. We were singing Duran-Duran songs on the top of the climbing apparatus that looked a bit like a fort-house there was a bunch of us aged between ten and fourteen Sam and I were eleven by then and enjoyed hanging out with both the boys and the older girls in our group. We all decided to head for home and started walking up the road when we hear a party going on. There was music playing and a lot of laughter and giggling in one of the neighbors back gardens, so we all went to have a look through the wooden paneled fence. I could not believe it I have never seen so many naked adults in one place before and they were no pin-ups I can tell you, it was enough to put you of your supper. And they were carrying on with each other, loads of middle aged people with not a care in the world for common decency, drinking, dancing and flirting with each other and doing all sorts, some were even skinny dipping in the pool. Sam and I thought this was hilarious. I remember one of the boys we were with saying, "Oh my God, that's my mom" and one of the girls saying, "And that's my dad with your mom". Sam and I just turned and looked at each other and said while giggling, "That's not good". Then Nicky was saying that his dad had warned him that some of them around here were a bit funny. Nicky was a good Catholic boy he thought the whole debortuary was disgusting, he walked away making a cross with his right hand and kissing his cross that hung around his neck on its gold chain asking Jesus for mercy. I can only guess for these secular souls that were probably doing more harm to themselves than the pleasure they had most likely been striving for. Things like this didn't amuse him, which was one of those great qualities that he had about him. I guess it comes down to good parenting. Sam and I just thought it was the funniest thing we had seen yet. Some of the other kids with us weren't happy because it was their parents doing this, what a mess. I couldn't wait to go home and tell my parents everything.

As soon as Sam and I got home we were falling over each other to tell our parents what we had seen going on in the neighbors back garden. My mom was shocked and my Dad was in fits of laughter, he said, "I knew that Nicky's dad was trying to tell me something about some of our neighbors but I didn't guess this", my dad was creasing up.

He says. "You know Nicky's dad pulled me aside and was saying" (my dad tries his poor Italian accent out) "these people, neighbors they not all like us with family, they different, stay away, you good people, God bless you, just don't get involved with them."

My dad continues. "I had no idea that is what he meant I'll have to thank him next time I see him. They're wife swapping, keys in a bowl, bunch of people. Well Julie; you wanted English people more like you"

"Frank, we're leaving, we are not staying here another minute". My mother says this with slight humour in her voice because you can hear that she too can see the funny side. But does mean what she is saying, she does want to move now.

My dad responds "Julie, don't be silly we've only just got here and were going to be here at least twelve months yet".

"No bloody wonder the Indians wanted to move so fast, I bet it wasn't anything to do with the size of the house it was the bloody neighbors". My mom then starts to laugh, "We're still leaving though when the year is up".

I don't blame her, what woman in her right mind would let her husband loose in a neighborhood like this. By the end of that year there were a few marriages that ended because of those parties and some of those kids really did suffer with their parents splitting up. These hedonistic soirees even infringed on the children's friendships with each other because they were falling out at times over their parent's dramas. They weren't all like that in the neighborhood. My parents did make friends with some of our neighbors that were more normal, if there is such a thing as normal.

The winter in Pointe-Claire was an eventful one, it was the year we had the ice storm that shut all of Montreal down. We had no power for over a week and we had to live in our snow suits. Sam and I looked outside our lounge window that morning to find the whole neighborhood was covered in ice and was in a state of complete catatonic stillness. It looked like we had been frozen in time. The ice-age had returned overnight while we were sleeping. There was a peaceful beauty about it but also loneliness; all signs of life gone, hibernating deep beneath the earth waiting for a great thaw that would not come for weeks. Even our home was trapped in the silence and cold. The buzz of electricity that would hum around the house unnoticed until it was gone from our ears. There was no T.V. or radio because there was no electricity, there was no kettle or stove either all of these things add to the life of a house and only become noticed when they are silenced. My mother hunted through the kitchen draws to find batteries that would bring life back to the radio with desperate need for any news of our stark situation. There was no heating hence the snow suits that we wore continuously throughout the blackout. Lights were replaced by candles and t-lights that flickered in the cold air in the rooms offering very little warmth to the shivering souls, with hands reaching out for what heat the flames were willing to offer to these palms. Every night we made our way by taxi to the only restaurant in the mall, with our parents and the driver taking great care on the roads. We were so grateful for the heat of the taxi's radiator, even if it was too brief. We had to queue up with the rest of Pointe-Claire for hours. My parents said it was like queuing up for your daily rations during war time, which opened up discussions about the two Great Wars and how civilians survived during those times, while we ate our supper. Best of all there was no school and I have to say I needed a break I had been sinking in the French school and didn't know how much more of it I could take at times. I had even become suicidal. This was respite that I desperately needed at the time. Even though I was freezing cold and Sam and I had to sleep in the same bed every night with our snow suits on. We had exhausted every board game we owned and were falling in and out with each other about ten times in a day because Sam with all the intelligence in the world could not help but cheat, if she thought there was a chance she may lose. I was just relieved I wasn't at school.

By the spring time my parents started looking for a house to buy and at weekends we would sometimes go with them to see homes all over the Montreal area. My parents finally found one they wanted in Pincourt and they took us to go and see it one weekend. I was excited about it because I just wanted to move away from Pointe-Claire. I just had not taken to the area well at all which was probably because I had to attend a French School. My deep depression and shame of my failure even drove me to finish with Nicky. I just didn't feel good enough to be loved so I pushed him away and broke both of our hearts. For that I am sorry but no one could comprehend my pain, after all Nicky was in an English school because his older sisters had gone to an English school and he was trilingual. My life had taken a nose dive into deeper depths of despair that I didn't want to share with anyone; at best I would lash out in anger and with hatred. I now spent most of my time alone.

By the end of the school year our school guidance counselor Guy called my mom and asked if I would like to come back to school for the last two weeks. He said he thought it would be good for me to see my class mates before school broke up. He also asked if I wanted to go to summer camp with the school. The grade six children were all going on a trip for a week to a summer camp and Sam was going with them and they wanted to know if I would come too. I said I would go back to school as long as they didn't expect me to do any work, which they agreed to, and I said I would go with them on the trip as long as Sam was going. It was strange though, because I didn't feel comfortable there. I just didn't fit in, and I felt like a stranger in a world that was not mine. My class mates were good with me but I just felt out of place. Sam, on the other hand was a part of that school now and she did fit in and was thriving. I wasn't pleasant to be around either, because I was angry inside. I was angry because all I had achieved with my reading and writing in the English school had been undone because I had been forced into a French school. I was angry with the French people for doing this to me and I was angry with Sam for not being me and surviving this. I was angry for being trapped in this mind of mine and I was angry that I was trapped here in Quebec and had no choice but to go through it. My anger issues became more apparent when I went on the school trip to the summer camp. I was fighting with Sam all the time just because I was so angry with her, I felt abandoned. I was snapping at her and she couldn't do anything right for me. And I was sick of fighting with other children that didn't like us just because we were from England.

The summer camp adventure holiday was to be a memorable time for us all. Sam and I shared a room with another girl from our class. There were many outdoor activities that they had us all participating in. There was canoeing, rock climbing, abseiling, and adventure walks with a guide. It was a great experience for us both but due to my anger issues I was fighting with Sam quite a lot which not only effected her enjoyment of the trip but fellow students and teachers became effected too. Our camp was situated right next to a lake which they used for the canoeing and other water activities. Across from the lake was an Island which they would take groups over to for adventure walks. Sam and I were put in a large canoe together with many of our classmates and our teacher Louise. We all had to paddle as a team and in sync to get to the Island, for one of our adventure walks, but Samantha and I began to argue over how to paddle. The argument escalated to the point that we were now physically fighting, causing our vessel to sway out of control. Louise begged us to stop and at that point we almost tipped the canoe. The other students on board had become frightened and were angry with us as well and it was decided that we were not to be in the same canoe from then on. My constant pain about my life circumstances was turning into palpable anger and I was taking it out on the one I felt closest and safest to, Sam.

At night the French kids would put their music on their stereos that they brought with them. Remember the big rectangle Ghetto blasters with double tape decks, that's the eighties for you. And they would have British pop bands blasting out of these things. It didn't matter how French these children were they loved Duran-Duran, Boy George with Culture Club, the Thompson Twins and Tears for Fears to name just a few. It always amazed me that they all loved the English pop stars but hated us for being English. It would beg the question why do you hate us for being English? Yet love our English Pop Stars so much that you want to dress like them and sing their songs? They would actually try to emulate these Stars but still proclaimed their hatred for the English. This was difficult to reconcile with because how were they able to disconnect the two? Was this hypocrisy or a schizophrenic society?

It Was Time

(V.C.H.S. 1987)

(IX)

Courage is not simply one of the virtues, but the form of every virtue at the testing point.

C. S. Lewis

My paper is due in for Mr. Connolly on the book "Man's Search for Meaning". My fellow peers have managed to renegotiate with Mr. Connolly. The due date is now early February not bad for a bunch of misfits. The catch is we now have to write a longer paper to include both the books (*Anne Frank, the Diary of a Young Girl* and *Man's Search for Meaning*) that we have read and other works relating to the Holocaust. No prizes for who started those negotiations. I'll say one thing for this Moral Education class it has had me thinking about my own past with all of its monsters and Angels and the lessons it has given me. The Holocaust should be discussed and studied along with all other known acts of genocide and persecution.

It is the only way we can possibly learn from what we did wrong to hopefully prevent another. I want to write it all myself but I can't, I need Sam's help. I dictate to Sam what I want to say. She helps me with some of my wording and then once Sam has written it down for me I recopy it out myself. My conclusion is this:

Persecution, it starts with, us and them. The others are not us. And not as good as us, they are evil they are stupid. Any of us could become the others without exception. That is what happened to Anne and Victor and so many more. Throughout the history of mankind there has been this injustice, this evil. Where the faceless nameless, grave less many that have been persecuted remain unknown, unclaimed and no atonement given. We are all the same; we should never be allowed to believe other. To believe other is a lie and will lead us to do great evil.

By the end of ninth grade we are all to choose our major subjects for next year that would have an impact on what we would then be able to choose at college (CEGEP) like sciences and arts. For most kids this is an exciting time. We are all brought into the school Library. Mr. Farley and Mr. Giguere address us all about needing to choose wisely because they will have a large impact on our future in college and university. We have a list put in front of us that we need to fill in and that we also need to discuss this with our parents and have them sign off on them. Other teachers are here to talk to us about their subjects individually to help us have an understanding of each course available. Mr. Choi is here talking about chemistry which is his subject that he teaches. I'm thinking, I want to do chemistry, I want all the sciences. Sam was already filling in her form, she knew exactly what she wanted and I ask her could she help me fill in mine and help me pick. Her response to me is not what I was expecting.

She says, "Justine, I can't carry you any further this has to stop. Next year we will be doing subjects like chemistry and physics, two years from then were going off to college, what are you going to do? I can't keep on carrying you all the time and I'm not going to either. You're on your own now Jay, that's it, I'm done."

"Sam you can't do this to me. I am begging you don't."

"Justine it's for your own good, this can't go on any longer."

"I will never forgive you for this. I can't do it on my own. What am I supposed to do?"

"Sam, please I'm begging you."

"Hate me all you want but something has got to give here. You can't keep going on like this. For your sake it has to end."

I can't believe what she is saying to me. I feel like my whole world is crashing down around me. I can hardly breathe. I feel betrayed. What was I going to do without Sam's help now? We still have exams to finish. I flee to the girl's bathroom to gather myself and to think of a way out. Why would my sister who had protected me for so long all my life even, just drop me like that? And what could I do about it? How could I tell anybody that I needed help? Who would I tell? I decided to go and talk to Mr. Choi. I walk round to his class and he is standing outside his door and I say to him, "I want to do Chemistry next year."

He looks at me like, right cards on the table now no messing around.

"You want to do chemistry yeh, well I will make a deal with you Justine. You go and see Mr. Farley and tell him the truth that you need help and you are willing to repeat next year and work harder than you have ever worked before and get the best grades you can get and I will take you for chemistry the following year. Is that a deal?" He looks me straight in the eyes.

I respond by looking back straight in his eyes. "It's a deal Sir".

Truthfully I couldn't believe he had just said that to me but at the same time it was like my prayers had been answered. Someone knew my secret and they had the answers for me. I now knew for the first time what I needed to do.

Mr. Choi finishes our agreement. "Go and see Mr. Farley now and I will come and see him later myself. "

That is exactly what I did. Mr. Farley's door was open, his door was always open that was his policy to students. The only time it was closed was when he had a student in there that needed to speak in confidence and the rule was if the door was closed he was busy with someone and if we wanted we could wait outside until he was finished, but on this occasion it was open. I knock on the open door to let him know I am here, he is writing something.

He looks up and says. "Hey, what can I do for you Justine?"

I just come out with it. "I can't read and I can't write not to any level that would make me literate anyway. I have spent the last three years hiding behind Sam and I can't do it anymore. I'm tired of it and next year I'm supposed to be doing things like chemistry and physics and I can't go on like this. I need help and I want to repeat the year on my own without Sam being there for me to hide behind. There I said it, can you help me?"

Larry Farley sits back and says. "Wow you certainly did say it. In all my years I have never had a student say this to me that they wanted to repeat a year and get help that is something else; you are something else, well done. Please come in and take a seat Justine."

I walk in and sit down and say, "I'm sorry for not telling you all the truth before and not getting help but I didn't even know how to and I was scared that you would... I don't know really. I was just scared of been taken away from Sam and not been able to stay here. I just didn't know how to tell anyone really".

Farley then says, "well, you have done it now and now it's up to us to help you and we will, don't you worry about that and I am so proud of you for having the courage to come forward and say something as difficult as that. You should be very proud of yourself Justine."

I wasn't, I was ashamed, scared and felt so vulnerable, I felt like a cheat, pride is not an emotion I feel.

"Mr. Choi made me a deal, if I confessed and got help, that next year, if I do well he will take me for chemistry. So here I am doing this, not just because of his deal but because I am so tired of hiding and not being able to read and write properly like all the other kids, I hate it. I hate my dyslexia; I hate my brain that has failed me. I am so sick of it controlling my life. I don't even know if I can learn to read and write properly but I am willing to give it a try and not lean on my sister any more. She's sick of it too, she's told me. She has had enough and I think it will do me good to be away from her and stand on my own two feet for a change".

Mr. Farley, "Justine you are a bright girl you will learn and I think you are right, it will do both Sam and you good to be apart for a while. It will give you both some time out and a chance to be recognised as individuals, it will be good for both of you."

I then say to Larry, "Sir how come your not mad at me?"

He smiles at me with that soulful smile and says, "How can I be mad at you? It takes great courage to do what you have just done and we owe it to you to help you, but it did have to come from you. You have come a long way in three years believe me and well done."

Mr. Choi turned up at this point and I turn to him as he leans against the door frame and say, "I did it, he knows now".

Mr. Choi, "Good, doesn't that feel better? A weight has been lifted of your shoulders that you have been carrying for so many years."

I get up and leave them both to talk. I needed to find Sam and tell her what I have done.

Looking back I realise that they knew the whole time what was going on and they were sowing the seeds to get me to that point, to do what I needed to do for me and Sam. I was never alone they were waiting for me to be ready to take these steps.

I find Sam with Kim, Karen, Laura, Tina, Bernadette and Dana upstairs in the hall way next to Sam's locker I just went straight up in front of everyone.

"I have done it, I told Mr. Farley everything and Mr. Choi says that if I do well next year he will take me for chemistry so that's it I'm going to repeat the year."

Sam looks at me and says, "Dusty, what did you do?" Sam always calls me Dusty when she is being more affectionate or wants my attention on a subject.

I respond, "What you wanted me to do. I told Mr. Farley and Mr. Choi..."

Sam's responds, "You told Mr. Choi?"

"No Sam he already knew, he made a deal with me, that's all and he told me to go and talk to Mr. Farley." I defended quickly.

The other girls at the locker start to ask questions now Kim says, "err, hello, what is going on here guys? What don't I know?"

I respond back, "I need help with my reading and writing more and I'm going to repeat the year to get the help I need."

Kim shouts, "You're what?"

Like she is my older sister and I just told her I'm knocked-up.

Kim continues, "What the hell are you doing that for? You can't leave the gang and drop down a year, no way"

Like it's her decision to make and that I have not thought of the consequences or the effect it will have on the gang because our year is too close and can't cope with one of us leaving. It's funny when I was making the decision to get help and stay behind a year it never occurred to me to consider my friends because this whole time it was me living in this hell alone there was no one else here with me not even Sam. She wasn't in my hell she was just there when it suited her hiding me, protecting me but she wasn't me, I was all alone. I say to Kim and the other girls "look I'm sorry you're disappointed with my decision but I have made it, I'm repeating the year because I need help and that is it." Sam says she is proud of me and completely understands and she hugs me and so does Karen, mind you Karen just loved a good hug any old hug, but I think they are both behind me on my decision. Kim and Laura are not so happy they believe I am making a big mistake and that I will not have any friends in the year below. That to me is the least of my worries, getting to grips with my literacy issues and pulling up my grades is the most important thing. After all I had just done the most difficult thing in my life and that was to admit the truth of what was wrong with me and ask for help.

The next day in the afternoon the usual gang of girls that Sam and I hung out with were sunbathing on the grass out in the front of the school grounds, while watching the boys playing base ball and I broached the subject again and said, "is it really going to be that big a deal with me repeating the year and not being with you all?"

Laura replies," yes it will Jay because you won't be graduating with us, you won't be at our grad dance or doing any of those things with us".

"Try and see it from my point of view, I need to do this for my sake. I can't go on anymore like this. I'm sick of it. I wouldn't be graduating anyway and I still might not if I can't get to grips with French." Why was I explaining my decision?

Laura, "You won't be able to hang out with us anymore."

Then Sam snaps back, "Yes she will that will not be changing."

Kim who was engrossed in watching the boys play ball, while soaking up the sun wearing her jean shorts that she has managed to roll up as far as she can along with her T-shirt that she has tied into a knot all in aid of getting the most out of the sun rays, whilst leaning back on to the parched grass beneath us, supported by her elbows in a very relaxed yet sophisticated manner, sporting her black Ray-Ban sunglasses, turns to look at Laura with disapproval. Her raised eyebrows and silence alone makes her stance on the issue quite clear.

Laura argues back, "But you will have no friends in the year below you're on your own."

Just as she says this, three girls from the year below us come walking up to us, Carol-Ann, Annette and Tina.

"We've just heard the news that you're staying back next year and going to be put with us. We think it's great and we want to be your friends, so you have nothing to worry about Justine we will be there for you."

I can't believe it the timing is perfect. I say to them, "how did you guys know?" And they reply, "The whole school knows everyone is talking about it even the teachers because they have never had a student choose to stay back before and ask for help." I'm kind of shocked and embarrassed but it is out there and I can relax now. Kim then turns to me and says, "Justine if this is what you need to do then do it, we're right behind you." She turns back to watch the boys play base ball that is the final word on the matter. You see to Kim, Sam and I, are not just her friends we are her sisters and what Kim says goes when it comes to this school. I was going to enjoy this summer because the biggest weight has been taken off me and I have no summer school, I have a whole summer of doing nothing but hanging out with my friends and having fun.

Back in the spring of 86' my mom decided she was going to do something about the law Bill 101 that had stopped her English daughters from having a proper education legally. She sat down one afternoon at the breakfast bar in our kitchen and started writing a letter to the new Minster of education, Claude Ryan because a new government had gotten into power and they were Liberals. Liberals were more sympathetic to the English and it did feel like there could possibly be hope for us and also for Quebec in staying with Canada and working out their political issues of language and rights. She would sit there composing her arguments while having one of her Moore cigarettes, as she would become more engrossed in what she was writing sometimes her cigarette would just burn out on its own, in the yellow stained glass ashtray that she had brought with her from England that had been in her life since the sixties before even her twinnies had graced her life. My mom was like a dog with a bone she would not let it go. When it came to her children and this issue of Bill 101 she was the big pit-bull protecting her two little baby pit-bulls. And when they didn't reply to her after several months of her waiting she wrote more letters and she told them exactly what she thought of their laws that were preventing her children from an English background from having an education in their native tongue.

I remember my dad saying to her' "Julie you can't write this you're incriminating yourself, for heaven's sake don't tell them you're breaking the law and have managed to get your children in a school illegally that is crazy".

But she didn't care she said she had had enough and was willing to go to prison; she wanted a fight about it basically with the government.

François said to her, "Julie we're not supposed to tell anybody about them being in school illegally. What about the teachers and Giguere they could go to prison?"

My mom shrugged off what he had said by defending her position and precautions already taken,

"I'm not that stupid. I didn't tell them which school they are in and they can't trace them because they're not in any school system, technically my daughters don't exist in Canada now."

In the letters she argued that soon we would need to be made legal so that we could get our high school diplomas to be able to move forward with our lives and that children hiding in the system would be graduating without them and that was not fair on the child. She also argued that there were many more children in Quebec hiding in the English schools just like her daughters so that it was a bigger issue than just two children and that they should realise that they had failed their own children of Quebec. She stated that she had to break the law to save her daughter that was severely dyslexic and that they tried putting me into a French school but that it had caused me arrested development and emotional problems. That I did not have the skills to learn French sufficiently to be educated in it and that their law did not accommodate for children that were dyslexic like her daughter, nor did it show compassion towards children with learning disabilities. It was a crime against humanity. When my mom finished writing, all that she needed to say, she then waited and waited some more. She was patient, then after many more months which by now had been a year she called Mr. Claude Ryan's office and spoke to his secretary.

The secretary said to my mother. "We all know who you are Mrs. Réussite everybody is talking about you and your letters you're pretty famous around here."

My mom replied, "Oh really ay and why is that?"

The secretary, "Because they are changing the law because of you Mrs. Réussite. All children who have been in the English school system illegally will be given an amnesty along with the schools and the faculty so that the children can graduate and receive their diplomas. So well done, you did it. When your daughters go back to school this year they will be legal and any children that have graduated this year illegally will now be able to get their diplomas."

This was the summer before we all grew apart and went our separate ways. Looking back now I can see that one of the reasons we grew apart was because of the decision I had made about my education forced me to grow. It changed me and I started thinking about the people I wanted in my life now with me. They needed to be people that are on my side supporting and understanding me. This was the summer we also had that torrential rain that flooded Montreal in all of two hours; it was on Tuesday the 14 July. Sam and I were at a friend's house two blocks from our house at the time, while my parents were out shopping. I was worried about the family dogs that had been left outside in the back garden of our home, so I ran home in the rain that afternoon and I got drenched, it was like I had got in the shower with my clothes on. Later that night we heard from a neighbor that a man had drowned in his car on the Décarie highway because he didn't get out of his car in time. (It was later reported that the man had had a heart attack). That was a tragedy. The flood was just too quick no one could have predicted it. It was a strange feeling it left in me because life shouldn't be that fragile, but it is. To think that, the same storm that had taken a life, had left me feeling so alive and liberated by its power. It felt more like a baptism from the heavens. I felt cleansed afterwards and rewarded for trying to save our dogs, my parents had returned home just minutes before I got there.

Dana's house was the place to be that summer of '87 it was one party after another, sometimes all weekend long. Dana's parents had this beautiful house in Hudson it had a balcony on the inside that over looked the lounge and an open plan ground floor. We all just loved going over there. Her parents seemed pretty cool because they let us all hang out there and have parties and nothing ever seemed to get broken so we were always allowed back the next week. Looking back I realise Dana would spend some time getting the house ready for the parties at the weekends. She would go shopping with her mom for groceries and rent the latest movies on VHS like *Saint Elmo's Fire* and *Ferris Bueller's Day Off*, these films were part of the whole weekend experience at Dana's. Feeding all of us kids for the weekend it must have been quite the shop. On reflection I realise that when you are a kid you don't think about things like that, you just go in the fridge and get what you want, we had it good at Dana's. Derek and the other boys would come over on their mopeds (scooters) and have cases of two-fours laid down in the foot rest. Sometimes Sam and Kim would grab lifts with Derek and the other boys on the back of the scooters and go down to the local depanneur with them to get more beer, smokes and wine coolers for the girls. I do remember one of the nights at Dana's, the house was packed with teenagers, not just from our high school but also some from Mac Donald High and Hudson High, the music was blasting so much I think the house was vibrating and we had teen movies playing on the TV in the lounge which contributed to the party atmosphere. There were kids making out everywhere and playing drinking games and just having a great time. Scott had climbed over the balcony railings and was hanging off the balcony by his finger tips and ended up dropping right on Dean's groin, where Dean sat directly below the balcony at the bottom of the stair case. Thank God the second floor wasn't too high up. Luckily Dean had been drinking, so it numbed some of the pain but he spent most of the night saying to himself, "Oh my balls, my balls". Dean was the comedian in our year he was always up for a laugh and was always up for a party. This same night Derek chased Sam, Karen and me around with blown up condoms like they were party balloons trying to get us to touch the condoms or if nothing else get the condoms to burst on us, he would get us girls trapped in a corner and press one of these balloons of his, so hard against us it would burst, we would be screaming at Derek, demanding that he got the offensive balloon away from us, that's boys for you. These were the best days of our lives.

The pit parties in Hudson were of the same vane but they would have a massive bonfire going and Derek and the other boys that had scooters would bring us girls up on the back of their scooters along with the beer and wine coolers. The sand pits were without bathrooms, which is not good for girls. We would have to go into the woods in pairs to keep a look out for each other to take a pee in the bushes. Dean, Derek and the other boys would always shout out the worst derogatory things they could think of in our direction to unnerve us and make us feel even more uncomfortable. One of my favorites was, "be careful of the hole in the bush", which would have Sam and Dana peeing in clock wise fashion looking for the hole in the bush. Instead of movies playing in the background we would have a Ghetto Blaster playing the latest eighties tunes and even better the boys would tell us ghost stories and gruesome urban-legend tales, that back then we actually half believed and would have most of us girls scared out of our minds. This was the Summer Kimberly and I became good friends because she had heard what I had done at school about repeating the year and thought it was gutsy, so she made a point of telling me this at one of the pit parties and we became close friends after that. Kimberly was a girl that spoke her mind and was attracted to strong willed people and saw my decision as an act of strong will. We would always look out for each other at parties when it came to guys, if one of us had too much to drink we had a pact, drink messed with your judgment so we were not to leave each other alone with any guys, that way we weren't taken advantage of. The rule was the only person we should end up in bed with by the end of a great night out was each other (and by that I meant we shared a bed) because that's what true friends do for each other. If a guy tried to over ride that pact we had permission to smack the bloke, no matter how cute the other one of us thought he was, in our drunken state. These were great rules, and in all the time we hung out together we stuck to our rules and they kept us safe.

I started back at school that fall, with a new class with students I kind of knew, because they have been faces and names in the halls the past couple of years; so they weren't complete strangers. I walked into my new class and who walks in right behind me but Dean and I said to him, "what are you doing here?" Thinking that he had just walked into the wrong class because that is something he would do. And he says, "they fucking failed me, can you believe that shit". I could not believe it, I wasn't on my own, Dean was right here with me. Dean is one of the funniest guys I've ever known, he will brighten up your world when you're having a bad day at school. He's the mate in the cell right next to you after a great night out on the town, that's Dean. From that day on we sat next to each other in most of our classes. See life's not so bad and as promised my new three amigos Carol-Ann, Annette and Tina, there here too.

I was excited for the first time since Saint Jude School and I was looking forward to fighting my demons and learning to read and write properly. The school had brought in a new guy called Mike Kudzia; he was a teacher for students like me that needed more support. My time table had been worked out so that some classes I had were with him and other students that were struggling too, so we were together getting tuition as a class and I had some sessions on my own with Mr. Kudzia for one to one tuition. It wasn't easy, having to sit there in a class with a teacher on my own and read and write badly; especially as a teenage girl, it's already the most embarrassing time of your life, but I had to put my ego aside and remember that that is why he is here, to help me learn. It left me feeling naked with all of my disabilities and dyslexia out in the open with no one or anything to hide behind. I would stumble over every single word that had more than one syllable to it, by the time I had read a sentence filled with these multi syllable words I would have to read it again to figure out what the sentence was about, then I had to read it again after that, to try and make it flow like a sentence should. It was the fight of my life in many ways, to decode every syllable in every word and make sense out of it, then on to the next one and so forth.

Writing was another fight that was even harder than learning to read. My mind wrote faster with the thoughts that came flowing out of me, I wasn't writing as fast as my mind was saying things. My sentences would get jumbled up with each other because I would start to write a complete thought but as the writing continued I would have only written half thoughts, then have gone on to the next thought without completing my first. So my writing was a mess, of incomplete thoughts and the spelling was written any which way it came out at the time. I never spelt a word the same way twice and the syllables would get messed up with each other and before my thoughts had a chance to make the paper they would end up like a car pileup on a high way with multiple causalities and very few survivors, and even less hope of my thoughts surviving the multiple car crash. Spelling was an enigma to me; literally I am good at codes because I had a lifetime of cracking them, to be honest. I reckon I would have had better luck with an enigma machine than French back then, as that child I once was, battling through thousands of codes a day while the rest of the world around me sees just basic words and sentences. Mike Kudzia was a brilliant teacher, when he could see that I was becoming too tired from the reading or writing, he would say, "let's take a break and play some pool". He had a full size pool table in his special class room and all the kids loved coming in here. Mike was awesome, he made me feel safe. He wasn't like most high school teachers he was like my best friend, who would listen to what was going on with me. He never pushed me to work. If I wanted to work he would be right there with me, helping me every step of the way but if I didn't want to work he would not push it. His attitude was, it needs to come from me no one else could do this for me. His character was laid back and filled with goodness. He was great to chat to about anything and fun to play pool with.

Mike had me reading books suitable for my level, well close enough; they were designed for the reading age of a ten year old. The first book he had me reading was, *Stand by Me,* which is my favourite movie. But it was so hard if I hadn't already known the story I would have been clueless of what I had read. I have the reading ability of a seven year old, stumbling through that book like a stammering idiot on every word and every syllable. He gave me the book to take home with me, to work on with my mom. I was going towards my locker with it stuffed up the back of my T-shirt so that no one could see what I was reading. Unfortunately, Sam had agreed to meet me for lunch and she was heading my way fast with Gerald in toe, a friend of hers who I didn't like that much because I always felt he was quick to pull people down with cutting remarks which just fed my fear of being teased. As I was hastily pulling the book from beneath my T-shirt, desperate to keep it concealed and put safely away in my locker, I could see them right behind me. I quickly tried to shove it in, but it was too late he had seen it. Gerald laughed and said, "You're reading a baby's book". My sister came to my defence by slapping him across the arm and glaring at him like she was fit to kill. He backed down quickly and left the subject alone. But its incidents like that that just knocks you. It's the little things that can kill you. Gerald was not a bad kid he was just like any boy his age. Full of hormones and a brain all messed up trying to rewire itself with the neural pathways shutting down faster that you can say "snap, crackle and pop" and the limited ability to only be sensitive to their own feelings. It wasn't his fault, that's just the way it is.

The truth is, once Mr. Kudzia gave me the tools I needed, I wanted to be set free and do it on my own and the day I said that to him in his class, that I wanted to spend the time in the library to work on my own, he was great with me about it. He just said, "It is up to you now, the fact that you have made that decision means that you are probably ready, but if you need me at all just pop in and I'll be there for you ok." I agreed and when I needed him I would go back, but it wasn't that often, once I had my foundations of breaking words down and building them back up again.

I would spend hours in the library reading anything and everything. I was a cup that needed to be filled with knowledge. I discovered authors from many generations around the world and I felt empowered by what I was able to read. I remember one of the first authors that I discovered in the school library, Samuel Clements, whose pen name Mark Twain is better known to the world. I found his structure and style of writing easy for me to read; there was a simplicity to it that allowed the stories to flow and they had innocence to them that in reflection helped me to relate. I fell in love with his stories and the characters. They fuelled my imagination but also they made me feel like I was not alone in the world that was at times for me over bearing and ignorant to children like myself. *The Adventures of Tom Sawyer* and *Adventures of Huckleberry Finn* helped me to escape into another world another time and learn about America through Twain's eyes and the characters he created. Samuel Clements was also very well known for his quotes but the one that has always stayed with me was the one he wrote about spelling and I have held it close to my heart ever since, like a child clutching hold of its favourite blanket. "I have little respect for a man who only knows how to spell a word one way." I guess for a dyslexic these words are golden.

I put the work in every day at home as well as at school. I would come home and sit at the breakfast bar in our kitchen and read to my mom while she made dinner. She would help me with my reading and home work. My mother gave me her pocket dictionary, that she had since she was a child. It was over a quarter of a century old and looked like it had seen better days and belonged in a museum. English is a living language therefore it was actually missing over twenty-five years of new words, like the word computer, but it was a life line to me none the less. It resembled my pocket sized New Testament the texture and fineness of the paper: ironically it was actually older and in many ways I treated it with the same respect. I took it wherever I went, it never left my side. I used it when reading to help me unlock newly discovered words and their meaning. However, when you are trying to find the spelling of a word it was not anywhere near as simple as just looking a word up, which would take seconds; I could spend half the night looking for the correct spelling of a word. It would drive me to despair some days. I had a tape recorder and would tape what I was reading to help me study. I dedicated time to each different subject I was doing at school. But French just would not stick, even with my little green book of douze mille verbes (twelve thousand verbs) I was just struggling, the language just would not penetrate my dyslexic brain. Between my brain and my mouth I couldn't even speak the basics, all the syllables just got mixed up in my head and would not come out right. It angered me to try so hard once more and just keep failing. I would listen to French radio and watch French T.V. I would even fall asleep with the radio on hoping it would somehow sink in and that by a miracle I would wake up and be able to speak French like everybody else. I even got a French boyfriend but that didn't help, one because that wasn't the type of French he wanted to teach me and two he would just speak in English to me, because his English was better than my French. Even Madame Palmieri would spend a lot of her free time, even lunch times tutoring me and it just would not go in. And I was so embarrassed because with me there was no proper foundation, even in English to work from because of my dyslexia, my English was so poor my French didn't have a chance. I remember Madame Palmieri saying to me that because I had so many holes in my foundations in English it was difficult for me to grasp the basics; even she struggled to help me. What she meant by that is, I had not been shown the basics in English with my verbs or how to conjugate them. I really only knew English from sound; and that was flawed with me. It felt like nothing would work, my mind was a jumbled up mess and was failing me; there was no saving me. In the end I gave up and just shoved the academic side of French under the carpet and hoped it would disappear.

I began to thrive in many other subjects though. I started to sit at the front of the class and I must have become a pain in the ass to most of my fellow classmates because I was so happy and enthusiastic about what I was learning. That year flew by quickly and because I had kept my end of the bargain so did Mr. Choi. I got to choose my subjects for secondary four; I chose Chemistry and Physics and I got accepted, life was getting better.

We were now legal and in different years so Sam took great pleasure in torturing the teachers even more by playing pranks on them. Sam started doing this particular prank back in secondary three, which was our last year together in the same grade, and the first time that they had separated us into different classes. She would get me to go into her class for her and she in mine; the teachers would not have a clue but all of our classmates would know because they could tell the difference. It's funny how kids can see more than adults sometimes, they spot the detail that the adult will miss. This was great fun, Sam had a hit list of teachers she was going to do this to and catch them out. She got every one of them. The teachers were ribbing each other about it in the staff room with whoever had been caught out. Saying "I wouldn't get caught out like that, I can tell the difference, call yourself a teacher and not see the difference between them". Bearing in mind that V.C. was a very small school, we were a family, not just a bunch of teachers and students pushed together for the next five years, like it or not; we were their children and they were our teachers. The best one Sam did was when she went into her own class for Biology and Mr. Grinham said to her,

"Now Justine, do you really think you have me fooled?"

Sam by this time took her usually seat in the class and looked at him in a curious way and the rest of the class was watching this, he then continued,

"I am not that easily fooled like the rest of these teachers. I have known you and Samantha long enough to know the difference."

The rest of the class hold their breath and wait for Sam to respond.

"Sir, you are so right, I apologise and I will return to my proper class and send Samantha back to you. Please don't be angry with me Sir, it was Samantha's idea, and you know what Samantha is like. She thought she could fool you and it didn't matter what I said."

The class says nothing and Sam leaves to go and get me from my Math class with Mrs. Gagnon and knocks on the door, enters and says,

"I'm sorry to bother you but Mr. Grinham has sent me back because he believes I am Justine".

Now what you need to know is that Mrs. Gagnon was one of the first of the teachers to get caught out and so had the worst of the ribbing so she says to Sam, "has he now, well then Justine, I think you should go and teach Mr. Grinham a lesson don't you?"

All the class was in fits of laughter they thought it was fantastic Mr. Grinham had fooled himself. So off I went, to Mr. Grinham's class and pretended to be Sam. Until there was only five minutes left of class then Sam walks back in and says,

"So you can tell the difference between us Mr. Grinham."

The class was howling with laughter he was well and truly gotten. It was a long time before the kids of V.C. let him live that one down. He would walk down the halls and one of the students would say, "There's no fooling you, hey sir." That is what life was like at V.C. we were forever playing pranks on each other, teachers and students alike because we were a very happy family.

Secondary four finally came around for me. I had made it up that mountain and got the subjects that I had applied for. My first day in Chemistry class Mr. Choi introduced the subject and the Chem. lab to us students. He explained to us, that in order to stay in his class that we had to sit a test on the Periodic Table of Elements and that we needed to get a hundred percent on the test, to be able to stay. We only got three attempts at the test and if we failed it after all three tries, we would have to leave. That scared me, because it meant I needed to be able to spell correctly, every single one of those elements and know their weights and correct abbreviations for them, no mistakes. My heart sunk, could I possibly do this? He then went on to say, that there were some students that probably shouldn't be here but he was giving them a chance and that to make it through the first month they would have to work harder than they had ever worked before. All the class looked at me, as he is saying this. I sink down in my chair and wish I had not dared to be here.

Mr. Choi went on to say, "There are some of you here that will go on to do great things. You will go to university and move forward with your lives academically and be happy with your lot in life. "

"Some of you will fail your first semester of college and not even get to university, and what you will learn here won't affect your lives, and you will get basic jobs in this world, like ones where you ask the question, Would you like fries with that meal sir?"

Again everyone looked at me. I just wanted the bell to ring now, and save me from the condemnation of them all. What was I thinking? A dyslexic, learning-disabled like me, that couldn't even speak properly? The bell rang, thank the Lord, I had been saved. The class filtered out and I tried to get out fast but Mr. Choi stopped me. "Justine, can I have a word?" The remainder of the class looks and sniggers at me, the boys mainly. I said, "Yes Sir". With my head bowed low, because I was expecting more of what had already been served to me in front of my peers.

"Justine, when I was saying those things in class I didn't mean you and I am sorry that your peers thought that I was. You need to know you earned your place here and you should be proud of that fact".

I lift up my head, to hear what he is saying to me, in disbelief.

Mr. Choi continues, "You are not much different than your sister. You also have the ability to go to university and make something of yourself. You just need more help and more time. It will come, but you do need help to get there, so you will have to come to see me twice a week, at lunch hour for half an hour sessions with me. Is that all right with you?"

I looked at him and smiled just a little, "yes Sir, I will, I promise".

I sat that Periodic Table of Elements test three times, but I past on the third go, I was in! Not everyone did though, some had to leave. Every Wednesday and Friday Mr. Choi tutored me. It wasn't easy but I got there, thanks to him and a lot of hard work. Mr. Choi spent a lot of time and patience getting through to me the basics of chemistry. I remember the first time he introduced to me the Mole, which is a unit of measurement in chemistry. Bearing in mind, that I had just spent the last year decoding the world around me in the written form and now I needed to decode the world of elements. Chemistry is the world in its truest most detailed form, where its language is formulas and mass. This was exciting to me but also very puzzling at times. Mr. Choi used to say to me, "I know when it is starting to sink into your brain, because your just like your sister, you start to chew your gum slower, I can see your brain turning it around, then a light bulb goes on and your there." Mr. Choi had faith in me and if ever I slacked off, and my grades started to slip he would tell me straight. He never pulled a punch, when it came to dealing with me, he would pull me back on track with a quick fast tug on my academic lead.

When it came to pranks, the one Mr. Choi played on Sam in her final year was the best of them all. You see Sam had played many a different prank on different teachers over the years. Mr. Choi had to endure her stink bombs that would empty a school. When she was confronted by him, Sam argued that his evidence against her was weak and therefore no case to answer to, which of course rattled his cage. Even my English teacher Mr. Colley had to endure Samantha's interpretation of Romeo and Juliette, "If Romeo had been a French Quebecquois man". She wasn't even in my class at the time of the prank; she was in an adjoining room that was merely separated by sliding doors. She was listening to my class reciting Shakespeare and she thought it would be funny to respond to Juliette before the student who was supposed to be reading aloud, but as a French man. So as the student is reciting "Romeo where for art thou?" in a monotone voice that was begging me to sleep. Samantha, bangs loudly on the sliding wooden door in a rapid repetitive demeanor like that of an angry neighbour to get our attention, then shouts out "phoque (Fhawk) you Juliette, I'm trying to get some sleep tabarnac." In a very heavy French accent with a firm tone of annoyance in her voice; this caused an absolute uproar by all the students in the English class, including the teacher. Clearly her passionate and fresh interpretation of a classic was performed far better than the student that should have delivered the appropriate next line. She always got away with it, even when she got caught out because they said her pranks were genius.

Sam had fallen asleep in chemistry class as per usual and instead of Mr. Choi doing his usual, of throwing chalk at her head or an eraser if she was snoring, he decided to get all the students out of the class and out of the school, but not just his class but every student in every class, so that it looked like school had finished and every one had gone home and left her. I was in physics class at the time and he came in and said to us all and our teacher, "quick Sam is asleep, you must leave quietly". We all got up as quietly as possible, like little mice. All of us left the building and then waited for the bell to ring and wake her up, which is what happened. Now to the outside world driving by, they must have thought that we were having a very quite fire drill, with all the students outside on the front lawn. Sam wakes up, wipes the drool of her face and takes a look around and notices that there is no one there in her class and that it is very quiet. She picks up her books and walks out into the hall and comes to realise she is all alone. She is thinking, oh my God, they have all left me. She is stood in the hallway swearing and shouting, she can't believe the whole school had left her and gone home, but then she hears a faint giggle that is trying to contain itself coming from the chemistry lab and she calls out, "Is that the laugh of a China man? You bastard what the hell is going on?" There was Mr. Choi he had been hiding behind one of the counters in the Chem. Lab and had just stuck his head slightly out of the door to get a glimpse of Sam because he just wanted to see the look on her face when she realised everybody had gone. He then begins to double up in stitches of uncontrollable laughter. The rest of us kids, hearing him laughing and Sam cursing, all run back into partake in our roll of laughing at Sam's misfortune.

The end of my sister's final year came around and I remember a friend of Sam's called Henri, from the French high school that we shared the campus with; turned up at our school one lunch time. I saw this gorgeously fit and very tall young black man coming through the front doors, as Sam and I were heading to the girls toilets and I said, "Sam, that's your mate Henri, what's he doing here?" Sam walked up to greet him with a great big hug and kiss. Henri and Sam were dance partners and trained in modern dance together over at his school. She seemed to know all the kids from that school, and was friends with them all. He explained to us that he had failed French miserably because he was dyslexic; that meant he was not able to graduate and get his high school diploma. Despite the fact that he had passed his English and the rest of the subjects with high grades, he was still going to fail. So he had made an appointment to meet our Principal and Mr. Farley to enquire about coming here next year to try and finish high school. Henri's ability to speak English and French was very good and you could not see any difference between the two languages. He had been raised in a French family he was born French, so to me this was a shock. I said, "What do you mean you failed French, you are French?" I felt my heart just sink. And he said his dyslexia had made him really suffer academically. Sam's face changed as we were talking and she said to him, "Darling, you can't go to an English school because you're French and you have always been in French schooling and so has all of your immediate family. Also Hun, the test that we sit here are exactly the same test written by the same school board, they are no different. I am so sorry, you will have to jump province to get your high school diploma. I am sorry." She then gave him a big hug. He said, "Are you sure?" She said, "I'm afraid so". He went to the meeting anyway and Sam waited for him to come out. He said as he emerged deflated from the meeting, "You were right Samantha, to be able to get my diploma I will have to jump province." She never did see him again after that, none of us did.

Grad year came around for me and Sam was gone. She had moved forward with her life at John Abbot College, down the road at Sainte-Anne-de-Bellevue. I was on my own now, with only my year left and the friends that I had made on my own. Everyone was talking about Grad; it is what every child dreams about from the first day they start high school. I wasn't, I had made no plans, and I avoided the subject because my issues with learning French were ticking away like a time bomb. I had tried my best for the past couple of years to forget it, but it was eating away at me to a point where I was losing sleep over it. By now my French teacher Mr. Ranger had given up teaching me French and had decided that the best thing he could do for me was teach me business, in French, because he told me I was going to be a business woman, so he taught me everything he knew, but with one condition, it must be taught in French. He had been doing this for the past two years when all the other kids in class had French work to get on with. He spent the time showing me everything I needed to know about running and buying business, and how to spot a bad one. So, thank you, Mr. Ranger, you were right and you taught me well. But it didn't make my problem go away, about not being able to graduate with a diploma like my peers.

It was my final months in high school and one morning on the Monday 12 of March 1990, a letter addressed to me turned up so I opened it, it was from the school board. Remember all that academic French I had been sweeping under the proverbial carpet, it was now a great big mountain and was about to flatten me. I was not going to be allowed to sit the French exam, so that was it, I could not graduate.

When I received the letter from the school board, stating that I was not going to be allowed to sit the French exam because I would negatively affect the bell curve, I remember feeling like I had been taken to the top of the mountain and shown the world below and been told this could all be yours but because I had failed French; due to my stupid mind and my dyslexia, I had been dragged back down that mountain and told I am sorry but you can't have it, you can't have any of it, because you're not good enough for us. I decided it was time for me to leave Quebec. I realised that there was nothing left here for me. I didn't belong here, no matter how much I tried, my life here was over.

My mom had booked a ticket for the sixteenth of March for a short visit to England to see friends and family. I said to her, "Mom I am taking your ticket, I am leaving and I am not coming back. I will go and live with Nan and granddad for a while until I figure out what I want to do. I've already called them and they are expecting me and granddad said he will help me get into an English school and finish my education over there, so I am going. I've had enough of trying over here; now I can't take the French exam there's no point me staying here. Can I have your ticket and do I have your permission to go?"

"Let me think about it," was her response. Maybe she was in shock and didn't know how to respond, I don't know? I didn't want to think about it anymore. I went to my room and started to pack. My mom came to my room and said, "Do you really want to do this?"

"Yes, it's time, there is nothing here for me. I'm not good enough for Quebec. I don't fit their criteria. I can't even get a half decent job in the service industry by law because I can't speak good enough French. I can wash dishes in a restaurant, that is my lot. But am I willing to do that for the rest of my life? No. I didn't learn to read and write just to end up working as a dish washer. I need more than that. I need to be able to go to college if I want and be like other kids my age and have jobs in retail or bars making better money. I can't do that here. I want a life that allows me hope of a better future. Mom, I can never have that here. Dyslexics like me don't have a place in Quebec it feels like there are laws against us; I feel there are laws against me. I am eighteen next month, literally in four weeks and when I fail again because of French; I am on my own. I am not a child anymore. I did all I could to pass but I am sinking still. Please mom let me go and find a chance at a better life".

I packed two suitcases of clothes and stuff I wanted to take with me.

That night I stayed at my sister's apartment and went out with her and her friends in Sainte-Anne's drinking and just in my own way said good bye to Quebec and the people. That night one of the guys from John Abbot college, that I had been seeing on and off for awhile, since Sam had started college there, came back with us to Sam's apartment and he was complaining about his course that he didn't really want to be doing it, I remember saying to him, "I would give my right arm for your problems right now. Try walking in my shoes for a change." I continued my rant at him, "You can at least change your course next semester. It's not that big a deal, so stop your whining." I left him to sleep on the couch and in the morning I woke him up gave him a cup of coffee, some paper and a pen and said "it's time for you to go to college and be grateful you have one to go to and don't just piss it up a wall, it's your life, I know, but, it's a great opportunity you have believe me, I don't have the same, so go." I walked out of the apartment and I walked all the way back to my school; on my travels I took in my neighborhood for one last time with all the memories it held for me. I went into my school and I asked Mr. Maisonneuve if I could just say a few words to my class mates. I walked into my class and stood before my friends and fellow students, for a second, I just looked at them all, their faces, and breathed in, like I was taking in my last image of them; I then blurted out. "I have loved sharing my last three years with you. Thank you all and I will miss you." I could feel my throat start to swell up and my voice was breaking so I cut short what I wanted to say and I left before I started to cry. I didn't give anybody a chance to change my mind or talk to me about it. I had made my decision and that was it. My sister and her boyfriend drove me to the airport that afternoon. In my pocket I had the letter from the school board, saying I wasn't allowed to sit the exam and I took it out and read it one last time as the plane took off and I put my jacket over my head and cried. Apparently my dad drove straight to the airport to stop me but the plane had gone, I had gone. The ticket said Mrs. J Réussite and my passport had Miss J Réussite on it, none of the airport staff noticed and I made it through with my mother's ticket. I didn't look back no matter how painful it felt. I knew I needed to do this for me, to give myself a chance at something in this world.

My grandfather kept his word, he took me to King Edward's, a grammar school in Sheffield and we met with the headmaster there. The headmaster said he would take me in and see how I managed. As long as I settled in and depending on the teachers' reports, I would be able to sit my "A" levels there. I had a week in the school and the headmaster called another meeting with me and my grandparents. He said I had impressed the teachers so far and was fitting in nicely, they were happy to have me in the school. Then my grandfather said it, "You wouldn't believe that she was dyslexic, would you, with the brains she has?" I just sank, I thought, God no; I could see it in the headmasters face. I wasn't going to be able to stay here. The next day at school the headmaster called me into his office and said, "Justine, I am afraid you can't continue here, you won't fit in, I am very sorry." I replied, "This is because of my grandfather telling you that I am dyslexic, you don't think I can do it." He responded, "Children like yourself cannot sit "A" level exams it isn't possible, you need a course more suited to you. I am sorry but it's no good us taking you on, for you only to fail, when it comes round to the exams at the end of the year." I was devastated, after all these years England hadn't change one bit; they were still a bunch of bloody bigots. I left and felt that I had once again failed and this time let my grandfather down.

Michael Came to See Me Today

(X)

For those who believe, no proof is necessary. For those who
don't believe, no proof is possible."

Stuart Chase

Five years later my life had moved on in another direction and
by the time I was twenty three I owned my own businesses
with my partner Jeff. One of the businesses was a gun shop in
Abridge in Essex, which I ran with an assistant and life was
relatively happy. I didn't have too much to complain about. I
owned my own house and had become a black belt in Tae
Kwon Do and ran my own Tae Kwon Do club. I had managed
to make a good life for myself here in England after all. I was
in my gun shop in Abridge one afternoon and a mysterious
man came into my shop, accompanied by a younger and much
taller man. He was about five foot six, he had blond hair and a
beard. He looked like a man in his sixty's and probably a cross
between an older version of Mr. Descent and Mr. Hastings.

He wore a hat that matched his greenish woollen suit, his entire outfit from head to toe made him look like he had just walked of a field after a morning of shooting game. I remember he had a walking stick in his right hand but I don't recall that it was a stick that he needed to use as an aid.

I said to him, "can I help you sir?"

He replied, "No Justine I have come to help you."

I was taken aback and replied, "Oh how is that then thinking he was probably a sales man that knew my partner, Jeff".

He then said as he walked towards me, "I came to help you Justine." He smiled and said, "Let's talk."

He guided me through into the smaller middle room while he did this my shop assistant stayed with his companion. This man had Rev. Farley's gentleness about him. His being was so peaceful it was like he was peace incarnate and he was charming and made me feel secure with him. Usually around men I have to keep my guard up, but not with him his mere presence allowed me to relax and be myself.

I said to him, "so what is this about?"

He replies, "It's about what is going on with you Justine."

I responded with, "oh really ay, and what is that?"

"The anger and frustration with your life is eating away at you. And how life has turned out for you, how you are dealing with things now, you are allowing a monster to grow inside of you."

I quickly reply, "Ok and what do you know about my life?"

"I know you are angry with how you have been treated and angry because you had to leave Canada. You're angry because you're here and not doing what you dreamed of doing. You're angry because you didn't get to finish your education; that you feel it was taken from you and you are angry at the world for taking it away from you. Justine, anger comes from frustration and fear. You are afraid of the world, you are afraid that you have let yourself down because of your dyslexia and you are scared people will dismiss you because of it."

He continues. "To deal with anger and fear you must ask yourself three questions.

"One, what am I afraid of?"

"Two, why am I afraid of it?"

"And three, what can I do about it?"

"Whenever you face fear or feel angry or even hatred about something you must break it down into its most basic form, fear and ask yourself those three basic questions. You will then be able to conquer your fears and therefore conquer your anger and hatred.

"How do you know this about me?"

He replies, "Justine, I have known you all your life and I have watched you."

Now this should have freaked me out but it didn't because I knew he was speaking the truth to me. He talked to me about the real me, my childhood and things that only I knew no one else, not even my twin.

He said to me. "Justine, you will go back to college and you will do your "A" levels, you will learn Psychology and you will study English Literature, just like you have always wanted and life will now move forward for you."

I said to him, "I can't go to college, they won't have me. I'm dyslexic."

He smiles at me, "Justine, you will go back now, they will accept you, nothing will stop you now. I promise you that. You will go to college and learn and move past this."

I said, "I can't, what about the shop and my businesses?"

He just smiled at me again and said. "They will do fine without you. Trust me, it is time. It is time now for you to move forward. Now that we have had our little talk, I can already see that you are back on track where we need you. I must leave you now but remember what I have told you."

I didn't realise it but we had been talking for sometime all alone without any interruption. He then started to walk back into the other room, the young man that was with him just turned and walked with him towards the door.

I said, "Wait. Don't go. I don't even know your name sir and you know mine."

He smiled and said, "Its Michael, but you can just call me Mike." He then turned to walk out the door.

I shouted out in a panic, "Wait, will I ever see you again?"

He smiled at me and said, "Justine, if you need me just call out to me, I will be there".

I replied, "Will you be there if I need you?"

He just smiled and said, "You won't need me again, not like this but I will always be there Justine."

He turned back around and he walked out of the shop. I stood in my shop just in awe of what had just happened, then I ran out of the shop to go after him but he was gone. In just a second he was gone, like he had vanished. This man had just come in and taken away all my hate and all my anger and gave me back my hopes and dreams and then he was gone and I didn't even get to thank him.

That night I laid in my bed thinking of the entirety of what Mike had said to me. He knew me. He knew a secret that I had kept inside of me for many years. I had never told a living soul.

"Let it go Justine, you don't need it. Just let it go."

"I can't." Tears start to swell up in my eyes; my throat feels constricted with the weight of my deep shame and my own tears that need to escape me. I look down at the rope in my hands and the white chair I had brought down with me to my parents' basement.

"You can, it will be alright. You don't have to do this, I am here for you."

"Why is this happening to me? I have worked so hard for this." The tears are now free-falling down my face. I clench the rope tighter in my hands. "

"I know you did but this won't fix it, just let it go and I promise everything will work out."

"I don't know how to survive this?"

"You will. I'm here with you."

That night it was Michael that stayed with me while I cried away some of my hopes and dreams. He stayed with me all through the night and watched me while I slept.

Michael had whispered in my ear that afternoon in my gun shop. "It was me that was with you, talking to you in the basement in your darkest hours, I was with you all through the night watching over you. I have always been here Justine."

Once more, I cried for that child and my dreams but now knowing I wasn't alone, Michael had always been here with me. I kept that secret with me until I had my son, only then did I finally share it with my sister and truly set that part of my soul free. Secrets eat at you like cancer; they steal little bits of you away over time, until your soul crumbles under the weight of the sin that isn't even yours to be carrying.

The next week I went down to my local college in Ashford in Kent where I lived and enrolled to do my "A" Levels and two years later I came out with two "A" Levels, Psychology and English Literature and a GCSE in Math as well. They were not the only treasures I came away with, I came away with friendships that will last a life time and now I could go to university if I wanted. Going back to complete my education taught me more than what you can ever read in books. It taught me that life is all about the climb. It's not just about who gets to the top of that mountain first. It's the individual journey that we all must take in our lives and they can't be compared to anybody else's climb up that mountain. We each have our own individual struggles and demons that we must battle. Sometimes even monsters disguised as people must be fought, for us to survive this world but we will grow stronger for the experience even the most unpleasant ones. We all have something to give to this world and it is our destiny to find out what that is because we are all God's children.

Many years later, now that I have a child of my own. I have done what I can to get him to embrace other languages, French being the most important to me but also other languages too like Spanish and Dutch. I remember my son Callem and I were in Holland one day in a department store and there was a play area for the children. Callem went up to this child and used all that he had in his acquired language skills to communicate with him because he wanted to make friends. He said, "Ike hate Callem, comment allez-vous et comment tu t'appelle" (my name is Callem, how are you and what is your name?) bless him; he just threw any and all language he had at this kid because he just wanted to make friends with this child. The mother of the boy smiled at us both and she said "well done he tried" he was three years old, I was so proud of him. The boy looked at him like he was from another planet at first but within a few minutes they were playing and of course more children came along and he tried the same with them. Children want to make friends and want to be able to communicate with other children and if they are not inhibited like me by a learning disability, they will embrace it all. I will continue to help myself to try and learn French, every so often I just go at it and I will continue to encourage Callem to learn French and many other languages. I speak to him in French with the little I know and at night when I put him to bed, I say to him, "Je t'aime et bonne nuit et fait dormir."

Conclusion

By

Samantha Flower

You must be the change you want to see in this world

Mahatma Gandhi

When any individual is subjected to persecution this negative energy often infects the persecuted. When looking at organized terrorist movements such as the FLQ who believe to be the victims of persecution and oppression and hold themselves out to be soldiers fighting against this injustice they are in fact infected by this. They unknowingly and unwittingly become conductors of this negative force that has entered and passes through them and back onto their oppressor, from which it comes full circle. It is this unbridled retribution which takes many innocent victims. Martin Luther King and Mahatma Gandhi lead their people through peaceful retaliation of oppression. When faced with the full brutal force of the oppressor they were spiritually and emotionally wise enough to choose peaceful methods. Instead of being inflicted by the evil that had done them so wrong and refused to be possessed by it. Not allowing it to work through them. How an individual chooses to deal with evil is a testament to one's soul. One becomes both victim and host when you choose to fight it with violent acts of retaliation or retribution through reversed oppression. Evil is a powerful negative energy that is all consuming and finds life in retribution. Those of us that choose peaceful methods to oppose the persecutors have refused to give this energy continued life for the greater good of their fellow man. This story illustrates how a child like Samantha momentarily becomes the conductor of this force in her retaliation against the oppressors when she tries to kill her teacher. However it also demonstrates for us an example of a peaceful resolution when she becomes more self-aware, where she offers the hand of friendship to the French child that has been taught to hate her. Which begs the question? Behind every revolutionist, freedom fighter or terrorist, is there a tortured child that does not realise that they have become infected, the blinded host unknowingly doing the devils work?

Mr. Pierre Trudeau dreamt of a Quebec that would be officially bilingual and by nature of its existence multilingual and multicultural. He did not want the French to be assimilated into the English, nor the English into the French. It was not his wish for Quebec or Canada to be homogenous in both language and culture. He also recognised the Native Americans, their languages and cultures and that of the allophones from all over the world that enriched the country. They are an important part of the history and continued growth of this new world. We can see this clearly in his speeches such as the "Proclamation Ceremony, April 17 1982" and "Official Language Bill, October 17 1968", what troubled Trudeau was that the majority of the people of Quebec did not understand his dream of how Quebec and Canada could be. I know this with certainty because I was very fortunate to have met this great man in the summer of 1994 on my way to get my bosses lunch. I had just turned the corner off Saint Catherine and there he was walking towards me, accompanied by a woman. In my excitement I called out to him, my face must have lit up like that of a Christmas tree. He loved to meet with students on the streets of Montreal and speak with them at length about politics and life. He told me how he felt that his own people did not understand his dream of what Quebec could become that he never wanted for there to be a reversed oppression onto the English. He did not want for a society that made anyone a second class citizen he had hoped that Quebec would become a place where all people were equal and had equal opportunities, judged by their contents of character and abilities not by language, ethnicity, religion, class or for the colour of their skin. It was a dream that he felt he would not realise in his lifetime and this grieved him. He recognised that the French people of Quebec were too bitter to this day about the years that they had felt oppressed by the English and all he could do was hope that a future generation could heal this in time and that it would pave the way forward for what Quebec could become. He asked if I would be entering into politics and possibly become the future Prime Minister. Sadly I said no, because one day I would be going back home to England my country of birth and I felt that my future was not in Quebec. He was surprised and saddened by what I said; he felt that Quebec could do with future politicians that shared his dream.

More than thirty years on from when this story began we still live in a world of fear, hatred, bigotry, prejudice and ignorance. Persecution continues in many forms and further acts of genocide have been committed against our fellow man. Quebec is under the watchful eye of international organisations that monitor potential threats of genocide. This is because of the shockingly cruel treatment of the Native

Americans of Quebec. Which may surprise some readers but this is a fact. The issues of its past are alive and festering today. The United Nations needs to also take a good look at the militia group, Milice Patriotique du Quebec (MPQ) because they have declared the Canadian military and the federal government their enemy. They have stated that Quebec is now a country, when in fact it is a Province, and they bear arms to protect themselves against foreigners.

The Bill 101 was never adapted for the needs of children with learning disabilities, no such exemption clause exists. I shall quote from the speech of Mr. Pierre Trudeau, which he gave on the day of the Proclamation Ceremony April 17, 1982. The day that the Canadian Constitution came home, he states this of the Constitution that was being proclaimed that day, *"....We now have a Charter which defines the kind of country in which we wish to live, and guarantees the basic rights and freedoms which each of us shall enjoy as a citizen of Canada. It reinforces the protection offered to French-speaking Canadians outside of Quebec, and to English-speaking Canadians in Quebec. It recognizes our multicultural character. It upholds the equality of women, and the rights of disabled persons..."*

The French people of Quebec cannot send their children to an English school if they so desire, nor can the English speaking immigrants, nor the allophones that become Canadian citizens. And of course, there are no exemptions for the learning disabled children of either. This lingualism (which is a form of racism) has been indoctrinated into the Province, contradicts the Canadian constitution and is in breach of the United Nation's Declaration of Human Rights. How did the Canadian Constitution allow the rights of parents, children and the disabled of Quebec to be lost? We are a species that claims to be so intelligent, yet so glaringly ignorant of how we can cripple and destroy our fellow man, even the most vulnerable.

We need to address our fears and show them the light as Michael advised Justine. What are we afraid of? Why are we afraid of it? What can we do about it? We must ask these questions in order to one day be at peace with ourselves and each other. So that hate, vengeance, oppression, retribution, greed and the need for power to finally dissipate from our species. If each of us could answer those questions individually, we could make it happen. The V.C.H.S. motto "Tuum est", meaning "it is up to you".

Vaudreuil Catholic High school Flag

A picture given to me by Rev. Farley (which was made by his mother in-law for the school) as a part of the school's motto that life and learning continues long after school, offering hope for the future.

Justine age 10 yrs, taken from Mrs Meehan's class photo